LUTHER LIVES!

Preaching Resources for the 500th Anniversary of Martin Luther's Birth 1483-1983

John R. Brokhoff

LUTHER LIVES!

1262/ISBN 0-89536-571-5

PRINTED IN U.S.A.

*Dedicated in gratitude to my
unknown Lutheran ancestors
who brought the torch of evangelical
truth to the present generation.*

CONTENTS

SERMONS

PREFACE

In 1983 probably many books on Luther will appear in observance of his 500th birthday (1483-1983). They will probably reevaluate Luther as a biblical exegete, a theologian, a churchman, a family man, a reformer and renewer of the church. This book is prepared for busy parish pastors to provide resources for preaching on Luther, his teachings and work. This book proposes to give a rapid review of Luther's life, to provide illustrations involving Luther for sermons on Luther, to look at Luther as a preacher, to recall some important sayings of Luther, and to provide ideas for sermons from a series of sermons dealing with Luther and the Reformation.

The preparation of this book is based on the assumption that parish pastors will welcome background material and suggestions for preaching in observance of the anniversary. It is also assumed that most pastors will want to preach on Luther and seize the celebration as an opportunity to preach Reformation emphases. Some may wish to preach a Luther sermon one Sunday per month in the anniversary year, 1983. Others may plan a series of sermons on Luther during the month of October, a series of five sermons for the five Sundays of October, 1983. If a pastor chooses to preach only one sermon on Luther, he may decide to do it on Reformation Sunday, October 30, 1983, or on November 6, 1983 (All Saints' Sunday) because it is close to Luther's birthday, November 10, which falls on a Thursday. The subject for a united Reformation service embracing various denominations, a Festival of Faith, might appropriately deal with Luther. The anniversary celebration affords the church the opportunity to emphasize basic doctrines rediscovered by Luther: the Bible as sole authority in faith and life, justification by grace through faith, the priesthood of believers, Christian liberty, and the meaning of vocation.

Because I love Luther who has been my hero and idol through the years of my ministry, it has been a joy to prepare this book. As a child I began to admire Luther. A stained glass window next to the pulpit in my home church in Pottsville, Pennsylvania had an effect upon me. The window depicted a life-sized figure of Luther dressed in a pulpit robe, preaching with a finger pointing to a text in an open Bible. When pastor of the Church of the Redeemer, Atlanta, Georgia, I had the architect design a pulpit in our new church with a frieze around the top portraying the main events in Luther's life. On the lectern were carved Luther's words from *A Mighty Fortress*, "One little word shall fell him." It can easily be seen that I am a dyed-in-the-wool Lutheran which I hope no one will hold against me. A Lutheran was explaining to a non-Lutheran friend that "I was born a Lutheran, raised a Lutheran, live as a Lutheran, and expect to die as a Lutheran." The friend asked, "Man, don't you have any ambition?"

Without apology I submit this book of homiletical helps for preaching on Luther's anniversary. Luther himself would approve the idea because he did the same for preachers in his day. He prepared the *Postils*, Luther's expositions of the lectionary lessons. When in the Wartburg, he prepared postils for Advent and Christmas. Later he did a Lenten postil. The material was to help pastors prepare their sermons. Of all his writings he put the *Postils* on top of the list of his work. In a sermon he said, "The postil is the very best book which I ever wrote." May this book on Luther be the best I, too, have written.

A Man for All Churches

A Mini-story of Martin Luther

Without fear of contradiction, one can truthfully say that Martin Luther is more alive today than he was 500 years ago. On the 500th anniversary of his birth (born in Eisleben, Germany, November 10, 1483), most churches will celebrate his birthday and acknowledge their indebtedness to him. In 1983 a new film, "Where Luther Walked," prepared for the celebration, will be seen by many millions of Americans. A few years ago John Osborne's "Luther" was a Broadway hit.

Well might the churches celebrate Luther's 500th birthday, for most are to some degree indebted to him. Here is the man who rediscovered the truth of the gospel and fearlessly proclaimed that salvation is by grace through faith. He is the one that cleansed the church and gave her back to the people by translating the Bible into the people's language, revising the liturgy to give people an opportunity to participate and to sing hymns. To him we are indebted for the Protestant parsonage and a new emphasis on the rightness of marriage and the sanctity of the family. It was this man who put the sacred into the secular by making all noble labor a calling of God. Through his discovery of the biblical principle of the priesthood of believers, the plain, common believer could intercede for himself and others as a priest of God and serve the neighbor as a little Christ. To Luther we are indebted for helping us see that the Bible as God's Word is the final and supreme authority in matters of faith and morals. The pulpit was made central, and preaching became biblical once again. Is not any one of these reasons enough to observe his 500th birthday?

Luther is a man for all churches. When his followers were first called Lutherans, he protested that they were not to be known as Lutherans but as Christians, for he asked, "Did Luther die for you? No, Christ died for you." Luther was both the hero and the father of the Protestant movement. The Reformed (Calvinist) churches are indebted to Luther, for John Calvin, after reading Luther, embraced the evangelical faith. Out of his work came the

Presbyterian and other churches holding Calvin's understanding of the gospel. Likewise, the Methodist church is indebted to Luther, for both John and Charles Wesley, the spiritual founders of Methodism, had a conversion experience following the reading of Luther's prefaces to Romans and Galatians. The more radical groups of the sixteenth century could not have come into existence if Luther had not succeeded in his fight for religious liberty. Even the Roman Catholic church can thank Luther for the reforms that took place in the Counter Reformation of the sixteenth century and Vatican II of the twentieth century.

Who was this man that accomplished so much for the church and society? One cannot understand nor appreciate Protestantism without knowing something about the Augustinian monk and Catholic priest, Martin Luther. Out of his life, thought, and experience with God came the Protestant movement.

One-Day-Old Christian

There was only one day in Luther's entire life when he was not a Christian. Because he was born on St. Martin's day, November 10, 1483, he was named Martin. His parents, Hans and Margarethe Luther, wasted no time in having him made a Christian. On November 10 he was born; on November 11 he was re-born as a Christian through baptism in St. Peter's church, Eisleben, Germany. When he was six months old, his family moved to Magdeburg.

Martin had a tough upbringing. His family was poor. Hans was a miner. For food Martin had to sing in the streets. His mother used to go to the woods to collect firewood. In home and school discipline was very severe. For Luther's stealing a nut, his mother beat him until the blood flowed. Once he ran away from home because his father beat him too hard. Luther related that for no reason at all his school teacher caned him fifteen times in one morning.

At the age of seventeen, Luther was matriculated at the University of Erfurt where, according to his father's wishes, he prepared to be a lawyer. At the end of four years, he earned his bachelor's and master's degrees. In 1505 Luther entered the graduate school to study law. After only a few weeks, he dropped out of the university and sought entrance to an Augustinian monastery in Erfurt. This radical change in his life was due to an experience he had while returning to the university after a vacation at home. A thunderstorm suddenly came up and a bolt of lightning knocked him to the ground. Terror stricken, he cried, "St. Anne, help me. I will become a monk." (St. Anne was the mother of the Virgin Mary and patron saint of miners.) By becoming a monk Luther felt he could avoid the wrath of an angry God.

After a few months, Luther's head was shaved and he was given the black garb of an Augustinian monk. After a year of probation, he was admitted as a full brother, and he took the customary oath of poverty, chastity, and obedience. With total abandon he engaged in the strictest asceticism of the monastery in order to please God and find peace for his soul. Later Luther remarked, "If ever a man could get to heaven through monkery, that man would be me." He fasted until his cheeks caved in. He persistently confessed his sins, often as long as a six-hour stretch. He appealed to the Virgin Mary and to the saints for help. He agonized over his sins and was constantly searching for a gracious God who would forgive him.

Luther's superiors in the monastery were so impressed by his piety and scholarship that he was ordered to prepare for the priesthood and was ordained in 1507. His first mass was a traumatic experience because he was overcome with the holiness and majesty of God present in the host. So great was his fear that he barely made it through the mass. The following year he was sent to Wittenberg University to lecture on moral philosophy for a year. Then he returned to the monastery to teach. In 1510 Luther and another brother were sent to Rome to represent their Order. In Rome he eagerly went from shrine to shrine and from church to church, but he became thoroughly disillusioned when he observed the luxury and moral laxity of both clergy and laity.

The Light Dawned

Upon his return from Rome, Luther was one of three new professors sent to Wittenberg University. Up to this time he struggled to find peace with God and to be assured of salvation. As a faithful servant of the church, he more than fulfilled all of the required disciplines of prayer, worship, fasting, and denials. He was under the impression that it was necessary to do good works to get right with God. He agonized in trying to find a gracious God who would forgive him. Staupitz, a fellow monk and close friend, urged him to study for the doctor's degree and to teach Bible at Wittenberg. Luther followed the advice. This forced him to study the Scriptures in preparation of his lectures. In 1512 he was awarded a Doctor of Theology degree. In his study of the Bible he discovered the life-changing truth that God makes a person righteous by faith alone and not by works. He learned that the grace of God could not be earned nor bought, but that it could be received as a gift accepted by faith. At last Luther had peace. It was a great enlightenment and he felt as though he were re-born. With this insight, Luther soon found himself in opposition to the church's teachings.

Sales not Souls

Having found the truth of salvation in the Scriptures, Luther became upset and enraged over the church's teaching and practice of selling indulgences for release from Purgatory and forgiveness of sins. The common people were led to believe that purchases of indulgences gained forgiveness. The church at that time taught that forgiveness depended upon penance. At the time of confession, the priest prescribed punishment for the sins confessed. If these penalties were not satisfied by the time of death, the person went to Purgatory to finish paying the penalty. Technically an indulgence was the Pope's reduction or removal of the penalty. But the common people believed indulgences could gain forgiveness of past, present, and future sins as well as reduce the time in Purgatory. The slogan encouraging the purchase of indulgences was —

> "As soon as the money doth clink in the chest,
> The soul it will flit into heavenly rest."

Pope Leo X announced a new indulgence which was publicized and sold by a Dominican monk, John Tetzel. The indulgence was granted to Archbishop Albert of Mainz to help him repay the loan of 10,000 ducats to the Fugger bankers and to finish St. Peter's Cathedral in Rome. Albert asked the Pope to allow him to be bishop of three provinces. For this special favor, they agreed on a price of 10,000 ducats. Since Albert did not have that kind of money, he borrowed the sum. Half of the proceeds from the new indulgence was to go to pay the loan and the other half was to go to the Pope. Luther objected to this practice of selling indulgences on theological grounds. He held to the biblical teaching that forgiveness was based on repentance which was a life-long experience in overcoming sinful desires.

On the eve of All Saints' Day, October 31, 1517, Luther nailed ninety-five Theses on the front door of the Castle Church. The door served as a bulletin board for the university. The Theses, written in Latin, were propositions in ninety-five paragraphs for the faculty to debate. The theme of the Theses was the present teaching and practice of selling indulgences. The sound of Luther's hammer was heard all over Europe, even to Rome.

Luther's hammer was heard all over Europe, even to Rome. The ninety-five Theses became the *Magna Charta* of religious freedom and the charter of the Reformation movement. Luther sent a copy of the Theses to Archbishop Albert who in turn sent them to the Pope. While the Augustinians defended Luther, the Dominicans condemned the Theses as heretical.

Getting into Trouble

At first the Pope ignored Luther's position, but later he summoned Luther to Rome for trial. Luther's prince, Frederick the Wise, who was Elector of Saxony, refused to allow Luther to be tried in Rome and insisted that the trial be held in Germany. In response, the Pope sent Cardinal Cajetan to confer with Luther in Augsburg. Cajetan failed to win over Luther who claimed that the Pope's word was not superior to Scripture as Cajetan maintained. Luther refused to recant his opposition to indulgences and now he went further by rejecting the Pope's infallibility in interpreting the Scriptures.

Later the Pope tried again to silence Luther. He sent Miltitz to undo the harm caused by Cajetan. Miltitz persuaded Luther to submit his case to a German bishop and to remain silent until the case was decided. He agreed to be silent as long as his opponents did the same. When they began to preach and write against him, Luther broke his silence.

The breach between Luther and the Pope widened as a result of an eighteen-day debate between Luther and John Eck at the university of Leipzig. In the course of the debate Luther declared that since the Pope was human, he was not infallible, that the councils of the church were subject to errors, and that the Bible was the ultimate authority. The result of the debate was Luther's identification with the heretic, John Hus, who was condemned and burned as a heretic for some of the same things Luther held. Judges from the university of Paris declared Luther's views to be heretical.

Use of the Pen

For one and a half years Luther's trial was delayed. During this time Luther used his pen and the printing presses to clarify his views. One of the major works was addressed to the German nation: "Open Letter to the Christian Nobility of the German Nation," in which he called upon the laity to do something about the abuses in the church. Another was "The Babylonian Captivity of the Church" which was addressed to the clergy to correct the sacramental system of the Roman Church. Probably his greatest work was "A Treatise on Christian Liberty" whose theme was a paradox: "A Christian man is a perfectly free lord of all, subject to none, and a Christian man is a perfectly dutiful servant of all, subject to all." In later years other writings were of monumental importance: the translation of the Bible into German, the Large and Small Catechisms, and his reform of the liturgy.

When the Pope's appeal to Staupitz, vicar of Luther's Augustinian Order, and to Frederick the Wise failed to bring Luther to recant, Pope Leo X and his advisers decided not to give Luther a hearing but ordered him to submit in sixty days. On October 10, 1520, Luther received the Pope's Bull (Notification) of Excommunication. It accused Luther of forty-one errors, demanded the burning of his books, charged him with heresy, ordered him to recant in sixty days, and threatened anyone who dared to give him aid and comfort. Two months later members of Wittenberg's faculty and student body gathered at Elster Gate outside the town for a bonfire in which they threw the books of Roman scholastic theology and canon law on which the Roman hierarchy based their authority. In a dramatic moment, Luther, with a prayer on his lips, quietly stepped forward to throw the Bull of Excommunication into the flames. Now Luther was considered an outlaw, an outcast, a heretic and no one was supposed to communicate with him or help him in any way.

Here I Stand

Though the Church excommunicated Luther, secular authorities did not arrest him. Luther's prince, Frederick the Wise, claimed that he could not arrest Luther or hand him over to church authorities because as yet Luther had not received a trial and therefore could not be considered guilty. Nevertheless, the Church called upon the State to carry out the Church's ban. The twenty-one-year-old newly elected emperor, Charles V, called a Diet to meet in Worms in 1521. Reluctantly the Emperor guaranteed Luther a safe conduct to and from Worms for the trial. Luther was brought before the assembly of prelates and princes. He was confronted with a display of his books and was asked to recant. He asked for time to consider the request. That night he spent in prayer realizing that his answer meant life or death for him. The next afternoon he returned to the Diet. Again he was asked to recant. He replied and confessed, "Unless convinced by the testimony of Scripture and right reason . . . I am bound in conscience, held captive by the Word of God in the Scriptures I have quoted. I neither can nor will recant anything, for it is neither right nor safe to act against conscience. Here I stand. I cannot do otherwise. God help me. Amen." On May 26, 1521, Emperor Charles V signed the Edict of Worms which placed an imperial ban on Luther for his heretical beliefs. By the time of the signing only four of the six princes were present to sign the Edict and only a rump Diet approved it. Luther was given twenty-one days to submit, his books were to be burned, and his followers prosecuted.

A Monk in a Castle

On his way back to Wittenberg, Luther was kidnapped by a group of friendly Knights and taken to the Wartburg castle belonging to Frederick the Wise. He grew a beard, dressed as a knight, and was known as "Knight George." For seven months the world did not know where Luther was. He occupied his time by writing letters, commentaries, and sermons. While at the Wartburg his greatest accomplishment was his translation of the New Testament into German.

Voluntarily, Luther came out of hiding because the Reformation was falling into the hands of radicals: Carlstadt, Zwilling, and the Zwickau prophets. There was violence, rioting, iconoclasm. Priests were beaten, vestments torn, altars and symbols demolished, and the liturgy repudiated. The radicals considered everything the Roman Church had was of the devil. The town council of Wittenberg asked Luther to return to restore peace and order. Early in December 1521, Luther hurried back to Wittenberg, for he considered what was happening to be far worse than anything the Roman Church had done to him. His return was incomparably brave, for there was no one to protect him from the Bull and the Ban. In a series of sermons he warned against rioting and rebellion. He condemned vandalism and held that unless it was specifically banned by the Bible, Roman religious aids and practices should be retained. He insisted that changes should be made only after the people were educated to the change. A Christian, he held, had a duty to be submissive to lawful authority. Luther was a reformer, not a revolutionary, and a conservative reformer at that! Because of his conservative stand, he lost the support of the religious radicals of his day. Under his conservative leadership, the preaching of the Word became central, people participated in the worship service, the liturgy was put into the vernacular, hymns were written (Luther wrote thirty-six), religious aids (church year, lectionary, vestments, symbols, altars, stained glass, etc.) were retained. Church polity became congregational and when disorder appeared, Luther called upon the princes, not as secular rulers but as Christians, to bring order out of chaos. This resulted in the state church of Germany.

A Conservative Reformer

Luther did not believe in revolution as the way to change the evil conditions in church and society. He opposed armed rebellion against the forces of law and order. He was against the use of force. His position: let the Word do it. Our responsibility is to teach and proclaim the Word, and God will make the changes.

As a conservative, Luther refused to support the nationalists: Hutten and Sickingen. They were super patriots who by force were out to get an independent Germany, free from the Pope and Emperor. At first the nationalists supported Luther's stand against Rome and offered him armed protection. Disagreeing with their method of force to get social change, Luther disassociated himself from them.

Luther's conservatism was manifest in his opposition to the Peasants' War. At the beginning the peasants saw in Luther their liberator from the economic conditons that enslaved them. They made their economic cause a matter of a religious war. When the peasants went out in armed rebellion, Luther took a stand against them and wrote a tract calling upon the princes to put down the rebellion. Though he sympathized with their grievances, he maintained that the Kingdom of God could not be brought on earth by military force.

Religious radicals gave Luther great concern. Among them were Carlstadt, Thomas Muenzer, the Zwickau Prophets, and Anabaptists. They were spiritual enthusiasts who placed primary emphasis upon the spirit. They repudiated infant baptism, banned the liturgy and the external organization of the church which they considered unnecessary and possibly the work of the devil. His opposition to them went to the extreme by agreeing to their destruction as heretics.

First Protestant Parsonage

In 1525 at the age of forty-six Martin Luther took a wife, Katharine von Bora, age twenty-six. She was one of a dozen nuns whom Luther helped to escape from a convent by their hiding in empty herring barrels which were hauled away from the convent. Since Luther engineered the escape, they came to him for help in starting a new life in the world. He was able to place all in a vocation or marriage except one, Katharine. She once let it be known that she would marry no one except Luther. In order to please his father, spite the Pope, and seal his teaching on the sanctity of marriage, he took Katie for his wife. It was a happy marriage resulting in six children. In addition they took in four orphans. To make ends meet, they also took students as boarders. The household had as many as twenty-five. It was a delightful family where love prevailed.

Continuing Controversy

From 1525-29 there was a series of Diets held to consider the Reformation which was spreading through Europe. Discussions were held to determine what to do with Luther the outlaw and how to overcome the spreading heresy. At the Diet of Speyer in 1529, Roman princes tried to stop, through a proposed resolution, the introduction of the heresy into new lands. Lutheran princes protested against the resolution. From this time, Lutherans were called Protestants.

In 1530 Emperor Charles V called a significant assembly in Augsburg. It was hoped that the religious division in the church and empire could be healed. Both sides were asked to present papers or confessions of their beliefs. Since Luther was an imperial outlaw, he was not permitted to attend and thus stayed at the Coburg castle. Melanchthon, Luther's close co-worker and colleague on the Wittenberg faculty, led the Lutheran delegation and wrote the Augsburg Confession consisting of twenty-eight articles showing how the evangelical teaching corresponded to the traditional church teachings and Scriptures. The Reformers went home without a victory, because Charles V rejected the Augsburg Confession, ordered Lutheran properties returned to the Roman church, and prohibited the sale of Lutheran literature. In 1531 the princes supporting Luther formed a military alliance to defend their faith from the Catholics. Armed conflict broke out after Luther's death in 1546.

The Ending at the Beginning

Luther continued to be active in the spreading of the Reformation by teaching, preaching, and writing. Three days before his death he preached his last sermon. He died in the town in which he was born, Eisleben. He was called there to mediate a controversy between twin brother princes of Mansfeld. Upon settling the dispute, Luther planned to return to Wittenberg the next morning. About midnight he became violently ill. As he was dying, a fellow-reformer, Justus Jonas, asked him, "Reverend Father, will you stand by Christ and the doctrine you have preached?" At age sixty-two, his last word was "Yes."

Thus ended the life of the man whom Roland Bainton claimed was "the renewer of Christendom."

Dates to Remember

1483 (November 10) — Martin Luther born in Eisleben, Germany
1501 — Entered Erfurt University
1505 — Entered the Augustinian monastery at Erfurt
1507 — Ordained a priest
1511 — Appointed professor of Bible at Wittenberg University
1512 — Received Doctor's degree
1517 (October 31) — Posting of the 95 Theses
1519 — Luther-Eck debate at the University of Leipzig
1520 — The Papal Bull of Excommunication
1521 — The Diet of Worms
1522 — Luther returned from the Wartburg to Wittenberg
1525 — Marriage to Katharine von Bora
1530 — The Augsburg Confession
1534 — Luther's translation of the Bible published
1546 (February 18) — Death in Eisleben

Luther Illustrations

Luther made much use of illustrative materials in his sermons to communicate the meaning of God's Word. He liked a good story or legend to get his point across. He used all kinds of homiletical materials. There were illustrations from nature: a snake had its life in its head, a palm is like the Bible in that it does not bend. His sermons abound in metaphors and similies such as:

1. The gospel is as intolerable to the self-righteous as the sun is to the night owl or wine to a man in a fever.
2. Works righteousness is as bad as feeding children to Moloch and Baal.
3. Who blasphemes the name of God is like a priest who feeds his pig out of a chalice.
4. To preach on a subject irrelevant to a congregation's needs is like speaking to a group of old maids on the merits of breast feeding.

Luther, moreover, was fond of proverbs; he had a collection of nearly 500 of them. Some of them:

1. "The Word of God is terrible to the fearful, fire to the ardent, oil to the meek."
2. "The world praises him who has done much, God him who received much."
3. "It is easier to make a bad man pious than a pious man better."
4. "Out of the same rose, the bee extracts honey, the spider poison."
5. "Though God promises to give, he nevertheless wishes to be implored."

On the 500th anniversary of Luther's birth in 1983, pastors will probably preach at least one sermon from Luther. From his own use of illustrations, Luther, no doubt, would encourage us preachers to use homiletical materials. Hopefully some of the following will be useful.

Courage

Luther describes his experience at the Diet of Worms where he confronted both church and state and was on trial for his life and his cause of the Gospel: "I stood in Worms, before the emperor and the whole empire, although I knew that the promise of a safe-conduct had been broken, and fierce hatred and deceit directed against me. Poor and frail as I was, my heart was so resolved that had I known that as many devils aimed at me as there were tiles upon the houses, I would have entered."

No Cause for Boasting

Once when Martin Luther heard a man bragging about how he "had accepted Jesus Christ as his Lord," Luther said, "Big deal! What are you patting yourself on the back for? If a rich man walks up to a poor man on the street and hands him a sack with a hundred dollars in it and that poor man then accepts the gift, think how absurd it would be for the poor man to go about bragging, 'Look at me! I was wise and good enough to accept a gift of a hundred dollars.'"

Who Lives Here?

One time Luther said, "If you should ask me, 'Who lives in your heart?' I would not say, 'Martin Luther lives here.' I would say, 'Jesus Christ lives here.'"

Discouragement

Luther was subject to periodic depressions. Often he became discouraged with the progress of the Reformation. There was a time when he was so discouraged that nothing anyone said could cheer him up. He went out of the house for a while. During his absence, his wife, Katie, changed into black mourning clothes with black veil over her face. When Luther returned, he was shocked and asked, "Who died?" Katie replied, "God died." Luther remonstrated, "Now you know that is foolish. You know God cannot die." Katie responded, "Oh, is that right? Well the way you were acting in desperate despondency, I thought for sure God died."

The Bible

A man very much interested in old books ran into an unbookish friend who had just thrown away an old Bible which had been stored in his attic. The latter explained that "somebody named Guten-something-or-other" had printed it. "Not Gutenberg!" gasped the book lover. "You idiot! You've thrown away one of the first books ever printed. A copy sold at auction recently for more than $400,000." Unmoved, the other man replied, "My copy wouldn't have brought a nickel. You see, some fellow named Martin Luther had scribbled all over it!"

Something Out of Nothing

Luther: "God created the world out of nothing. As long as you are not yet nothing, God cannot make something out of you."

Public Confession

In the Reformation period, Martin of Basle was convinced of the truth of the Gospel but was afraid to make a public confession of it. He wrote his confession of faith on a piece of parchment: "O most merciful Christ, I know that I can be saved only by the merit of Thy blood. Holy Jesus, I acknowledge Thy sufferings for me. I love Thee! I love Thee!" Then he removed a stone from the wall of his chamber and hid the parchment behind the stone. One hundred years later it was discovered. Contrast this confession with Luther who said, "My Lord has confessed me before men; I will not shrink from confessing Him before kings."

Conscience

Luther was summoned for trial at Worms, Germany, by Emperor Charles V in 1521. His writings were displayed and he was ordered to recant if he wanted to save his life from death as a heretic. Luther concluded his own defense with these immortal words: "Unless I am convinced by Scripture and plain reason — I do not accept the authority of popes and councils, for they have contradicted each other — my conscience is captive to the Word of God. I cannot and I will not recant anything, for to go against conscience is neither right nor safe. Here I stand. I cannot do otherwise. God help me. Amen."

Trust

Martin Luther was once told that his protector, Duke Frederick, was wavering in support of the Reformation and that he might abandon him. With concern a friend asked Luther, "Then where will you be, Martin?" Luther replied, "Right where I have always been — in the arms of the everlasting God."

Dying in the Faith

In 1976 there was discovered in a sixteenth century book a handwritten description of Martin Luther's death. It reveals that his death was not violent as his enemies claimed. In the

14

sixteenth century a violent death indicated that God permitted the devil to snatch that person's soul. The letter is as follows:

"At his final end a little prayer of Doctor Martin Luther.

"This morning the 18th of February around one o'clock Dr. Martin stood up from the bed and spoke to Doctor Jonas, 'Oh, oh I am in so much pain. I shall stay here at Eisleben.'

"As he went into the room, they warmed him. They he says, 'O heavenly God, you beloved Father of Jesus Christ, you have surely revealed yourself to me. I have recognized and proclaimed you whom the whole world and the godless calumniate and blaspheme, and this I know surely, even though from this life I shall be torn. I shall be separated from you beloved Lord Jesus Christ by no one. To you I commit my soul and also my spirit.' Three times: 'Lord Jesus Christ into your hands I commit.'

"Afterwards he says, 'Hear, hear out of the depths of death. You are a Lord over death and a deliverer in the midst of death.' Afterwards he says the words of Christ, 'God so loved the world that he gave his only begotten son.' Again he finally says, 'I am going.'

"And then spoke Doctor Jonas and Mr. Michael, 'Dear Doctor, with you is the Lord Christ. Do you intend to continue hanging on to him?' Then says he from the heart, 'Yes' and departed thereafter.

"A little prayer of Doctor M. Luther at his last end."

An Answer to Worry

During Luther's last days, his wife, Katie, was very worried over his health. While on his last journey to Eisleben, he wrote her: "You are worrying for your God as if He were not almighty . . . . Pray and let God do the worrying! You have never been ordered to worry for me or for yourself. It is written: 'Cast all your cares on the Lord, for he cares for you.'"

Conservative Reformer

While Luther was in hiding in the Wartburg castle as "Knight George," the Reformation movement got out of hand in terms of excesses: violence and destruction of church property and traditions. To straighten out the excesses caused by extreme radicals, Luther left the Wartburg to return to Wittenberg. By doing so, he subjected himself to immediate arrest and execution as a heretic by order of the State and excommunication by the Church. His action showed not only that he was a brave man but a conservative reformer who wished to keep all good things of the church not forbidden by the Bible. Upon leaving the Wartburg, Luther wrote to his protector, Frederick the Wise: "I am coming home. I am not asking you to protect me. If I thought you would protect me with the sword, I would not come. If the Emperor comes after me, do not stand in his way, though you need not hand me over to him of your own accord." Emperor Charles V did not come for him because he was too busy fighting the Turks, France, and the Pope.

When the Truth Broke Through

Luther explained how the truth of the Gospel came to him: "Night and day I pondered until I saw the connection between the justice of God and the statement that 'the just shall live by his faith.' Then I grasped that the justice of God is that righteousness by which through grace and sheer mercy God justifies us through faith. Thereupon I felt myself to be reborn and to have gone through open doors into paradise. The whole of Scripture took on a new meaning, and whereas before the justice of God had filled me with hate, now it became to me inexpressibly sweet in greater love. This passage of Paul became to me a gate to heaven . . ."

Doubt

Luther and a fellow-monk were sent to Rome to represent their Order. Seeking peace with God, Luther climbed the sacred stairs in front of St. John Lateran Church in Rome. It was taught that if one crawled up the twenty-eight steps on hands and knees and said the Lord's Prayer on each step, a soul would be released from Purgatory. At the top of the steps, Luther expressed his doubt: "Who knows whether it is so?"

Undesired Fame

Luther had no intention of becoming famous. His ninety-five Theses were written for only the faculty of Wittenberg University to discuss the current local practice of indulgences. The Theses were written in the language of scholars — Latin. The press got hold of the Theses and translated them into German, the language of the people. Like wildfire they spread and became the talk of Germany. Karl Barth compared Luther's coming to notoriety to a man in the darkness of the night climbing a staircase in a cathedral steeple. To keep from falling, he grabs a rope which rings the cathedral bell, awakening the whole city.

Salvation for Sale

The match that started the forest fire of the Reformation was the sale of indulgences. Luther nailed his ninety-five Theses on the castle church door at Wittenberg to debate the practice of selling indulgences among the faculty. Luther's prince, Frederick the Wise, had a collection of sacred relics in the castle church where Luther regularly preached. The collection had a total of 19,013 holy bones of saints and martyrs. An annual pilgrimage was made on All Saints' Day (November 1) to adore the relics. Those who came and made a contribution could receive from the Pope a reduction of 1,902,202 years in Purgatory for both the living and the dead. Frederick the Wise used the money to build a bridge across the Elbe river and to support the university and castle church. To question the indulgences was a danger to the economic welfare of the prince. At the same time across the border close to Wittenberg, a Dominican monk, John Tetzel, was selling a new indulgence for Archbishop Albert of Mainz and the Pope. Half of the money from the sale of indulgences was to go to Albert to pay off his debt of 10,000 ducats to the Pope for the position of archbishop and the other half was to go to the Pope to finish the construction of St. Peter's Cathedral in Rome. Each person who purchased an indulgence was guaranteed full forgiveness of all sins, both past and future, and an immediate release of dead loved ones from Purgatory. Tetzel's slogan was:

"As soon as the coin in the coffer rings,
The soul from Purgatory springs."

Laity to the Defense

At the Diet of Augsburg (1530), the laity of the Reformation came into prominence. The Augsburg Confession, a famous statement of Lutheran beliefs, was written by a layman, Philip Melanchthon. Being under the imperial ban and bull of excommunication, Luther was not permitted to attend the Diet to defend or explain his teachings. He was allowed to come as close as Coburg where he stayed in a castle. The lay princes came to the defense of the Reformation faith. When Emperor Charles V ordered the German princes to march in the Corpus Christi procession, they refused. George, the margrave of Brandenburg, bravely defied the Emperor: "Before I let anyone take from me the Word of God, I will kneel and let them strike off my head." In signing the Confession, the princes, like the signers of the American Declaration of Independence, pledged and jeopardized their lives and fortunes.

On Asking Foolish Questions

Luther was once asked what God was doing and how he occupied himself before he created the universe. He answered, "He was cutting switches with which to thrash inquisitive questioners."

What One Can Become

An old German school teacher had the custom of entering his classroom filled with boys with a gracious and condescending bow. One day he was asked why he daily bowed before his class as though the kids were his superiors. He explained, "No one knows what great thing one of these boys will do in the future." He was right, because in that very class there was a boy named Martin Luther.

Discovery of the Gospel

Luther explained how he discovered the Gospel: "Night and day I pondered until I saw the connection between the justice of God and the statement that 'the just shall live by faith.' Then I grasped that the justice of God is that righteousness by which through grace and sheer mercy God justifies us through faith. Thereupon I felt myself to be reborn and to have gone through open doors into paradise. The whole of Scripture took on new meaning, and whereas before the justice of God filled me with hate, now it became to me inexpressibly sweet in greater love . . ."

Victory Over Satan

One night Luther became aware of a terrifying, cold, sinister presence in his room. He turned over and saw the devil sitting there in the corner and he said, "Oh, it's you!" And he turned over and went to sleep. Luther said, "The devil is a toothless bulldog. He looks fierce, but for the Christian, he has no bite." In A Mighty Fortress Luther sang, "The prince of darkness grim, we tremble not for him. His rage we can endure. For lo, his doom is sure. One little word shall fell him." That one little word is Jesus.

Dependence on God

After Luther throws the Bull of Excommunication into the fire: "Oh, God! Oh, God! Oh, thou my God, my God help me against the reason and wisdom of the world. You must — there's only you — to do it. Breathe into me, like a lion into the mouth of a stillborn cub. This cause is not mine but yours. For myself, I've no business to be dealing with the great loss of this world. I want to be still, in peace, and alone. Breath into me, Jesus. I rely on no man, only on you. My God, my God do you hear me? Are you dead? No, you can't die. You can only hide yourself, can't you? Lord, I am afraid. I am a child, the lost body of a child. I am still-born. Breathe into me, in the Name of Thy Son, Jesus Christ, who shall be my protector and defender, yes. My mighty fortress, breathe into me. Give me life, Oh Lord. Give me life."

Relics at Wittenberg

Luther nailed his ninety-five Theses on the castle church door on the day before All Saints' Day, November 1. The problem of indulgences was not only in the next province where John Tetzel was selling indulgences but it was also right at home in Wittenberg. Elector Frederick the Wise was known for his collection of relics consisting of 19,013 items including a fragment of the crown of thorns Jesus wore and some of the Virgin Mary's milk. On All Saints' Day, veneration of these relics could earn a total of more than 500,000 years in indulgences.

Standing Alone for the Gospel

"Let my friends think me mad. The affair will not reach an end (if it is from God) unless, as his disciples and acquaintances deserted Christ, so all my friends desert me, and the truth is left alone — truth which will save itself by its own right hand, not mine nor yours, nor any man's . . . If I perish the world will lose nothing . . . I, unhappy, fear lest perchance I should not be worthy to suffer in such a cause."

What Luther Had to Say

In 1983 the Protestant world will be observing the 500th birthday of Martin Luther, born in Eisleben, Germany, on November 10, 1483. Though born a half millenium ago, his voice is still heard by many in the church. Below are some things Luther had to say that are as true and applicable today as they were 500 years ago.

About Assurance of Salvation:

"I have been baptized and I have the Word, and so I have no doubt about my salvation as long as I continue to cling to the Word."

It is said that when Luther had doubts about his salvation, he would crawl on his hands and knees to the baptismal font where God adopted him as his child.

About Jesus:

"Christ is the true treasure, the basis, the foundation, the sum total, to whom all are drawn and under whom all are gathered. So, he who does not find or receive God in Christ will never find him. He will not find God outside of Christ."

"He who doesn't believe in Christ can't be saved."

About the Church:

"Therefore he who wants to find Christ, must first find the church. The church is not wood and stone but the assembly of people who believe in Christ. They certainly have Christ in their midst, for outside the Christian church there is no truth, no Christ, no salvation."

"I ask that men make no reference to my name, and call themselves not Lutherans, but Christians. What is Luther? My doctrine, I am sure, is not mine, nor have I been crucified for anyone."

About the Scriptures:

"The cloths are nothing but Holy Scripture in which Christian truth lies wrapped up. For the entire Old Testament contains nothing but Christ as he is preached in the Gospel . . . The cloths are the sign by which one would know him. For there exists no other witness on earth to Christian truth but Holy Scriptures." (Luther held that the Scriptures were the manger that held Christ.)

About Faith:

"Faith is an acoustical affair."

"Christian faith is the utter submission to God's grace which is purchased for us and granted to us by the blood of Christ . . . Consequently, there is no repentance, no satisfaction for sins, no grace, no eternal life, except by faith alone in Christ, faith that he has given full satisfaction for our sins, won grace for us, and saved us. Only then can we do works freely and gratuitously, to his honor and for the good of our neighbor, not in order to become just and receive eternal life and rid ourselves of sin."

About the Power of the Word:

"The pope says, 'As I will it, so I commanded it, you must perish rather than resist me.' Therefore the pope, whom our princes adore, is full of devils. He must be exterminated by the Word and by prayer."

About Church Music:

"Next to the Word of God, music deserves the highest praise. The gift of language combined with the gift of song was given to man that he should proclaim the Word of God through music." (This quotation was framed and hung in a choir rehearsal room in Farmville, North Carolina).

"If any man despises music . . . for him I have no liking, for it is a gift and grace of God, not an invention of man. Thus it drives out the devil and makes people cheerful . . . Gospel means good tidings; of this we joyfully sing and speak."

About Christmas:

"There are three wonders here: one, that God should become a man; another, that a virgin should bear a child; and the third, that Mary believed. And the greatest of these is that Mary believed."

About Liberty:

"A Christian is the most free lord of all and subject to none; a Christian man is the most dutiful servant of all, and subject to every one."

About Love of Neighbor:

"I must even take to myself the sins of others as Christ took mine to himself. Thus we see that the Christian lives not to himself but to Christ and his neighbor through love." (Luther further held that a Christian is "a little Christ" to his neighbor.)

About Heaven:

Upon the death of his daughter, Luther said, "I'd like to keep my dear daughter because I love her very much, if only our Lord God would let me. However, his will be done! Truly nothing better can happen to her, nothing better."

About the Heart of the Bible:

"For this much is beyond question, that all Scriptures point to Christ alone."

"So we must cling to the pure Scriptures alone which teach nothing but Christ."

"All of Holy Writ points solely to Him, attesting that He alone possesses seal and letter."

"When Christ is not known, it is impossible to have any understanding of Scripture since He is the Sun and Truth in Scripture."

About His Depression:

"For more than a week I was close to the gates of death and hell. I trembled in all my members. Christ was wholly lost. I was shaken by desperation and blasphemy of God."

About God and Gods:

"If a man have no God, he must have an idol."

About Bible Reading:

"For several years I have read the Bible through twice in every twelve months. It is a great and powerful tree, each word of which is a mighty branch; each of these branches have I well shaken, so desirous was I to know what each one bore and what they would give me. And the shaking of them has never disappointed me."

About Happiness:

To a despondent prince Luther wrote: "God has commanded us to be joyful in his presence; he does not desire a gloomy sacrifice. Be merry with them; for gladness and good cheer, when decent and proper, are the best medicine for a young person — indeed, for all people. I myself, who have spent a good part of my life in sorrow and gloom, now seek and find pleasure wherever I can. Praise God, we now have sufficient understanding of the Word of God to be able to rejoice with good conscience and to use God's gifts with thanksgiving, for he created them for this purpose and is pleased when we use them."

About Insincere Christians:

"Perhaps God would rather hear the cries of the ungodly than the hallelujahs of the pious."

About Reward for Service:

For translating the Bible into German, Luther received not one penny. He explained why he did it: "I have done it as a service to the dear Christians and to the honor of One who sitteth above, who blesses me so very much every hour of my life that, if I had translated a thousand times as much more diligently, I still should not deserve to live a single hour or have a sound eye. All that I am and have is of his grace and mercy, nay, of his dear blood and his bitter sweat. Therefore, God willing, all of it shall serve to his honor, joyfully and sincerely."

About Word and Spirit:

"God will not give you his Spirit apart from the external Word. Be guided accordingly, for it was not for nothing that he commanded that his Word should be outwardly written, preached, sung, and spoken."

About Prayer in the Sacristy:

"O Lord God, dear Father in heaven, I am indeed unworthy of the office and ministry in which I am to make known Thy Glory, and to nurture and to serve this congregation.

"But since Thou hast appointed me to be a pastor and teacher, and the people are in need of the teachings and the instructions, O be Thou my helper and let Thy holy angels attend me.

"O Lord Jesus Christ, Son of the living God, Thou Shepherd and Bishop of our souls, send Thy Holy Spirit that He may work with me; yea, that He may work in me to will and to do through Thy divine purpose.

"Then, if Thou art pleased to accomplish anything through me, to Thy glory and not to mine or to the praise of men, grant me, out of Thy pure grace and mercy, a right understanding of Thy Word and that I may also diligently perform it."

About Reason:

"This I know; reason is the devil's whore, born of one stinking goat called Aristotle, which believes that good works make a good man."

About Use of Force:

When the knights of Germany led by Hutten offered their military protection and might to Luther, he in 1521 wrote to Spalatin: "I am not willing to fight for the gospel with bloodshed. The world is conquered by the Word, and by the Word the church is served and rebuilt. As Antichrist arose without the hand of man, so without the hand of man will he fall."

About Trusting in the Word, not Feeling:

"If you will not believe that the Word is worth more than all you see or feel, then reason has blinded faith. So the resurrection of the dead is something that one must believe. I do not feel Christ is risen, but the Word affirms it. I feel sin but the Word says that it is forgiven to those who believe. I see that Christians die like other men, but the Word tells me that they shall rise again. So one must not be guided by his feelings but by the Word."

About Personal Experience:

"It is not enough that you say Luther, Peter, Paul have said so, but you must experience Christ himself in your conscience and feel that is unquestionably God's Word, though all the world opposes it."

About One Truth Never to Be Given Up:

"We will not give up the liberty of conscience bound by any work or law, so that by doing this or that we should be righteous, or leaving this or that undone we should be damned. Since our opponents will not let it stand that only faith in Christ justifies, we will not yield to them. On the question of justification we must remain adamant, or else we shall lose the truth of the Gospel. It is a matter of life and death."

About Doctrine, not Ethics:

"Wyclif and Hus assailed the immoral conduct of Papists, but I chiefly oppose and resist their doctrine. I affirm roundly and plainly that they preach not the truth — to this I am called. When I can show that the Papists' doctrine is false, then I can easily prove that their manner of life, though something therein be amiss, will be pure also."

About the Meaning of Righteousness:

"I hated Paul with all my heart when I read that the righteousness of God is revealed in the gospel (Romans 1:16, 17). Only afterward, when I saw the words that follow — namely that it's written that the righteous shall live through faith — and in addition consulted Augustine, was I cheered. When I learned that the righteousness of God is his mercy, and that he makes us righteous through it, a remedy was offered to me in my affliction."

About the Making of a Theologian:

"Not reading and speculating, but living, dying, and being condemned make a real theologian."

About What Makes a God:

"To have a God properly means to have something in which the heart trusts completely . . . To have God, you see, does not mean to lay hands upon him in a purse, or shut him up in a chest. We lay hold on him when our heart embraces him and clings to him. To cling to him with our heart is nothing else than to entrust ourselves to him completely. He wishes to turn us away from everything else, and to draw us to himself because he is the one, eternal good."

About Faith:

"Oh, it is a living, busy, active, mighty thing, this faith. It is impossible for it not to be doing good works incessantly. It does not ask whether good works are to be done, but before the question is asked, it has already done them, and is constantly doing them. Whoever does not do such works, however, is an unbeliever. He gropes and looks around for faith and good works, but knows neither what faith is nor what good works are. Yet he talks and talks, with many words, about faith and good works. Faith is a living, daring confidence in God's grace, so sure and certain that the believer would stake his life on it a thousand times. This knowledge of a confidence in God's grace makes men glad and bold and happy in dealing with God and with all creatures. And this is the work which the Holy Spirit performs in faith. Because of it, without compulsion, a person is ready and glad to do good to everyone, to serve everyone, to suffer everything, out of love and praise to God who has shown him this grace." (Upon hearing these words of Luther read on

Aldersgate Street, John Wesley felt his heart "strangely warmed.")

About Music:

"Music is a fair and glorious gift of God. I would not for the world forego my humble share of music. Singers are never sorrowful, but are merry, and smile through their troubles in song. Music makes people kinder, gentler, more staid and reasonable. I am strongly persuaded that after theology there is no art that can be placed on a level with music; for besides theology, music is the only art capable of affording peace and joy of the heart . . . the devil flees before the sound of music as much as before the Word of God."

Luther the Preacher

Although Luther was a professor and a prodigious writer, he was foremost a preacher. He preached an average of four sermons per week. Today there are in existence about 2,300 of his sermons. His preaching went beyond the pulpit. When he taught, he preached, and when he preached, he taught. His writings were essentially sermons.

One of Luther's greatest contributions was in preaching. The pulpit was made central in the church. For Luther the preached Word was superior to the read Word and the administered Word, the Sacraments. Because of his teaching and practice, there was a return to Biblical preaching. In Luther's day little preaching was done by the local priest. The preaching was largely done by several orders of monks (Augustinian, Dominican, Franciscan, Benedictine) for the purpose of getting support for Crusades or for selling indulgences. The sermons were primarily ethical in content. They dealt with scholastic intricacies and details. Often the sermons dealt with irrelevant questions such as whether cut-off hair and finger nails would also be resurrected. For every point, church authorities were quoted. The emphasis was upon good works with asceticism as the moral ideal. The first sermons of Luther corresponded to the sermons preached at that time, sermons that today we would call topical or thematic. In 1521 a change came to Luther's preaching. He broke with the current practice and his preaching became biblical and expository.

Luther's Theology of Preaching

Preaching had top priority for Luther because of what, in his mind, preaching is. Luther's theology of preaching was based upon his theology of the Word. Preaching is of utmost importance because of the importance of what is preached — the Word of God. Luther claimed that preaching *is* the Word of God. It is extremely important, because the Word means salvation. In preaching, "It is God himself who speaks." A sermon is not what a person says about God but what God says to the people through the preacher's proclamation of the Word. Since no one is greater than God and since nothing is more important than God's redemption and revelation in the Word, preaching the Word cannot be excelled. This Word comes as both proclamation and deed. The Word is God's speaking his truth. Also, the Word is God's deeds, the greatest of which is the deed of Christ on the cross. Thus, to preach the Word is to preach Christ crucified. And where is the Word found? It is in the Scriptures, for the Bible is the recorded Word of God. The Bible is indispensable for preaching the Word, because it sustains oral proclamation and preserves the preaching of the Word from error. The Bible as the word is both Old and New Testaments, for the Word as Law and Gospel are in both Testaments. In the Old Testament the Gospel is there as promise and as fulfillment in the New. Consequently, preaching to be the true Word must be biblical, and a true sermon is an exposition, illustration, and application of the Word to life today.

Luther held that preaching was the oral Word of God. The Word comes to us in three modes: oral, visual, and written. The Sacraments are the visual Word, and, of course, the written Word is the Scriptures. Of these three, the original and most important is the oral Word. The written Word is a dead letter. The visible Word without preaching is sterile. It is the oral Word that makes the Word a living word of life and spirit. The Apostles were not called to write but to preach. St. Paul was commissioned not to baptize but to preach. In the preaching of the Word, listeners are confronted with Christ and through the Spirit, identified with the Word, faith is given. Thus, the preaching of the Gospel is God's way of saving sinners. That is the heart of the Gospel and because of it, preaching is essential, indispensable, and necessary.

Luther's Style

Luther's preaching was simple and clear. It was directed to the peasants and servants rather than to students and faculty of the University. He spoke from an outline and thus the sermons we have today are those recorded by his friends. He did not follow the traditional rules of Homiletics. When he ran out of time or text, he would abruptly stop. The strength of his sermons was in their content: doctrines and theology. He was a popular preacher because he dealt with life situations, used concrete illustrations and descriptive language. His messages were vigorous, blunt, creative, and authoritative. He was a fearless proclaimer of the truth in the text. Often Luther used direct address, and dialogue with the congregation or between characters in the text. Usually there was an adversary or opponent of the gospel. The sermon was a struggle between the good and evil forces. The people were called upon to make an ultimate decision.

One characteristic of Luther's preaching was biblical. He was an expository preacher. He always used a text which was announced at the beginning of the sermon, except when on days other than Sunday, he preached on the Catechism. He explained his method: "I take pains to treat a verse, to stick to it, and so to instruct people that they can say, 'That was what the sermon was about.' " His text was usually a passage (pericope). He spoke about the theme or main point of the passage and used it to unify his remarks about other parts of the text. The power and effectiveness of his preaching were in the Scriptures.

Also, Luther was a liturgical preacher. He preached within the context of worship, the church year, and the lectionary. The sermon was a sacramental element of worship. On Sunday mornings his texts were taken from the gospel lesson of the lectionary. His use of the lectionary for preaching shows modern preachers that lectionary preaching can be attuned to the times and can be dynamic enough to cause a reformation.

A third characteristic is his catechetical preaching. In his day the church was teaching non-biblical doctrines and the common people were almost totally ignorant of the Bible's teachings. As a result Luther felt it necessary to deal with the teachings of the Scriptures. Since he was primarily interested in the faith rather than in the morals of the church, he saturated his sermons with doctrine. Though his sermons were simple and clear, they were deep with profound biblical theology. Not only did he preach Sunday afternoons, Mondays and Tuesdays on the Catechism, but his Sunday morning sermons were teaching sermons on the basic doctrines of the Christian faith.

Luther's Contributions to Preaching

1. Luther revolutionized preaching in his day and set a pattern for generations to come by making preaching the top priority of the Ministry and the Church. To him the preached Word was more important even than the Sacraments. As the oral Word, preaching is the Word of God. There was a perpendicular dimension to preaching: God used preachers as his spokespersons.

2. Another contribution is his making Christ the center of preaching. The Word of God is the personal, incarnate Christ. He is the Word made flesh. The heart of the Scriptures is Christ.

To preach the Word is to preach Christ crucified. This was not the case in his day for he complained, "The world is full of preachers, but none of them preach Christ." In one of his sermons he thundered, "Nothing but Christ is to be preached."

3. Luther contributed a return to biblical preaching. He brought into general acceptance expository preaching. This was the taking of a passage from Scripture and expounding the meaning of it in relation to the daily needs of the average person. He did not attempt to preach his views on life or to give good advice derived from his personal experience. He let the text speak. The truth of the sermon was the truth of the Word. This enabled him to be a fearless preacher filled with conviction and confidence.

4. Luther, through preaching, deepened the ethical teachings of his time. His emphasis was not on the moral act but on the attitude and motive of the Christian. He considered gratitude as the highest motive of Christian living and service. Gratitude was one side of the coin while the other side was grace. He appealed for faith which is the receptive agent of grace. Grace is received by faith and faith is expressed in grateful service.

As a preacher Luther has what today's church needs. If preachers today are to bring a new reformation to the church and world, they would do well to emulate and imitate Luther in a fearless proclamation of the Word of God found in the Scriptures.

Luther on Preaching

Priority

"A minister is one who is placed in the church for the preaching of the Word and the administration of the Sacraments." (Table Talk, p. 100)

"You know that the greatest divine service is the preaching of the Word of God, and not only the greatest divine service, but also the best we can have in every situation . . . " (Sermons I, p. 232)

"Christ did not command the Apostles to write but only to preach." (Pelikan, Luther the Expositor, p. 63)

"You ought to lift up your hands and rejoice that we have been given the honor of hearing God speaking to us through his Word." (Luther's last sermon — Sermons I, p. 390)

"We hold that the Sacrament is less important than preaching." (Table Talk, p. 90)

Agony of Preaching

"I would rather be stretched upon a wheel or carry stones than preach one sermon. For anyone who is in this office will always be plagued; and therefore I have often said that the damned devil and not a good man should be a preacher. If I had known, I would not have let myself be drawn into it with 24 horses." (Sermons I, p. 222)

"If I were to write about the burdens of a preacher as I have experienced them and as I know them, I would scare everybody off. For a good preacher must be committed to this, that nothing is dearer to him than Christ and the life to come, and that when his life is gone, Christ will say to all, 'Come to me, my son. You have been my dear and faithful servant.' " (Table Talk, p. 73)

The Word

"The objectivity and certainty of the Word remain even if it isn't believed . . . I stake my soul on it and am ready to die for it . I put my confidence in no other faith, but in the Word of God." (Table Talk, p. 192)

When Luther was asked for permission to publish his collected works, he said: "I'd like all my books to be destroyed so that only the sacred writings in the Bible would be diligently read." (Table Talk, p. 274)

Jonas once claimed that Luther knew everything in the Bible. Luther denied it: "I know there are many things I do not know. I have preached for 25 years and still don't understand the verse, 'He who through faith is righteous shall live.' " (Table Talk, p. 287)

"In my preaching I take pains to treat a verse of the Scriptures, to stick to it, and so to instruct the people that they can say, 'That's what the sermon was about.' " (Table Talk, p. 160)

"I opposed indulgences and all the papists, but never with force. I simply taught, preached, and wrote God's Word, otherwise I did nothing. And while I slept or drank Wittenberg beer with my friends Philip and Amsdorf, the Word so greatly weakened the papacy that no prince nor emperor ever afflicted such losses upon it. I did nothing; the Word did everything." (Sermons I, p. 77)

Substance

"Preach one thing: the wisdom of the cross." (Sermons I, p. 14)

"Nothing but Christ is to be preached." (Sermons I, p. xx)

How to Preach

Luther was asked, "Reverend Father, teach me in brief how to preach." Luther responded: "First, you must learn to go up to the pulpit. Second, you must know that you shall stay there for a time. Third, you must learn to get down again." At first Cordatus was angry with the answer but upon reflection he realized that Luther was saying: first, a preacher must have a call to go up to the pulpit. Second, he must stay there to give pure doctrine. Third, he should not preach longer than an hour.

"Cursed be every preacher who aims at lofty topics in church, looking for his own glory and selfishly desiring to please one individual or another. When I preach here, I adapt myself to the circumstances of the common people. I don't look at the doctors and masters, of whom scarcely 40 are present, but at the hundred or thousand young people and children. It's to them that I preach . . . for they need to understand. Therefore, dear Bernard, take pains to be simple and direct . . ." (Table Talk, p. 235)

"He's the best preacher who can teach in a plain, childlike, popular, and simple way. I prefer to preach in an easy and comprehensible fashion, but when it comes to academic disputations, watch me in the university; there I'll make it sharp enough for anybody and will reply, no matter how complicated he wants to be." (Table Talk, p. 384)

"Postil is the very best book I ever wrote." (Sermons II, p. ix) Luther prepared postils to help preachers prepare their sermons. They were expositions of the epistles and gospels of the Lectionary.

Prayer and Preaching

"When you are to preach, speak with God and say, 'Dear Lord God, I wish to preach in Thine honor. I wish to speak about Thee, glorify Thee, praise Thy name. Although I can't do this well of myself, I pray that Thou mayest make it good.' When you preach don't look at Philip or Pomeranus, or me or any other learned man, but think of yourself as the most learned man when you are speaking from the pulpit. I have never been troubled by my inability to preach well, but I have often been alarmed and frightened to think that I was obliged to speak thus in God's presence about his mighty majesty and divine nature. So be of good courage and pray." (Table Talk, p. 157)

To God Be the Glory

"Whatever good we do in preaching is done by God; when we

preach, it is God's work if it has power and accomplishes something among men. If my ministry is profitable, I ascribe it to God. If it produces fruit, I do not glory in myself; this is not my work, but the mercy of God, who has used me as his instrument." (Sermons I, p. 224)

Qualitites of a Good Preacher

"A good preacher should have these qualitities and virtues. First, he should be able to teach in a right and orderly way. Second, he should have a good head. Third, he should be able to speak well. Fourth, he should have a good voice. Fifth, a good memory. Sixth, he should know when to stop. Seventh, he should be sure of his material and be diligent. Eighth, he should stake body and life, goods and honor on it. Ninth, he must suffer himself to be vexed and flayed by everybody." (Minister's Prayer Book, p. 422)

Reluctance to Preach

Staupitz, Luther's superior at the Augustinian monastery in Erfurt, had to persuade Luther to preach. Luther explained, "Under this pear tree I advanced 15 arguments to Dr. Staupitz; with them I declined the call. But they did me no good, when I finally said, 'Dr. Staupitz, you are taking my life; I won't be able to endure it three months.' " Staupitz succeeded and Luther preached until three days before his death.

Frequency

"Often I preached four sermons on one day. During the whole of one Lent I preached two sermons and gave one lecture every day." (Table Talk, p. 282)

Preaching in Luther's Day

"The reason why the world is so utterly perverted and in error is that for a long time there have been no genuine preachers. There are perhaps 3,000 priests, among whom one cannot find four good ones — God have mercy on us in this crying shame! And when you do get a good preacher, he runs through the Gospel superficially and then follows it up with a fable about an old ass or a story about Dietrich of Berne, or he mixes in something of the pagan teachers, Aristotle, Plato, Socrates, and others, who are quite contrary to the Gospel and also contrary to God, for they do not have the knowledge we possess." (Sermons I, p. 64)

(Before the Diet of Worms, 1521, Luther preached according

to the style popular in his day — a scholastic structure typical of the thematic sermon. After 1521, Luther developed his own style of preaching in terms of expository-catechetical preaching.)

SERMONS

Oh, for a Luther Today!

By means of his faith Abel still speaks, even though he is dead.
Hebrews 11:4 (TEV)

Next to the pulpit in the church in which I grew up — located in Pottsville, Pennsylvania — is a large stained glass window with a six-foot tall Luther, dressed in a pulpit robe and holding a Bible in one hand while pointing with the other to a text. Above his head is a scroll with the German words (originally it was a German-speaking congregation), "Ein Feste Burge ist Unser Gott" — "A Mighty Fortress is our God." On the bottom of the window are the words: "Martin Luther Geboren den 10 Nov. 1483" — "Martin Luther born Nov. 10, 1483." It is customary for a memorial to provide the dates of both birth and death. In this case only the birth date was given. Is this to say that Luther never died? Is he still alive today?

In our text the author of Hebrews claims that Abel, Adam and Eve's second child, though dead from the beginning of the human race, is still speaking to us by means of his faith. On this 500th birthday of Luther, we can say the same of Brother Martin of Wittenberg. But how, you may ask, can anyone speak relevantly to a world 500 years later? What does Luther know about current conditions, needs, and problems? Just as Abel or Jesus or Paul speaks to our times, so does Luther. It is possible because he speaks the truth of God's Word which is applicable to every generation. Through his deep and dynamic faith, Luther still speaks to us today.

In an age of theological confusion, declining church membership, rampant cults, and moral corruption, we need to hear Luther speak to our situation. Once Coleridge exclaimed, "Oh for a Luther in the present age!"

Speaking About the Bible

Luther lives today by means of his faith in the Bible as the Word of God. If he were physically present in our day, he would thunder against the misuse and abuse of the Bible by some Christians. The problem is the over-rating of the Bible to the point of Bibliolatry and Biblicism. Some have made the book a paper pope. It needs to be hastily said that no one, living or dead, had a greater love, respect, or appreciation for the Bible than Luther had. For him the Bible as the Word of God was the ultimate and only authority in faith and life. He considered the Bible to be preeminent over the Pope as the infallible vicar of Christ, the Councils of the church, the tradition of the church, the church fathers of old, and present day theologians. Because of this position, Luther got himself in hot water at the Leipzig debate with John Eck who pushed Luther to admit that he questioned the authority of the papacy and thereby was subject to the charge of heresy. At the Diet of Worms, Luther risked his very existence on Scripture: "My conscience is bound to the Word of God."

In our day Luther would have no part with the Fundamentalists who insist that the Bible was literally inspired and must be literally interpreted. For them the Bible is errorless not only in truth but in every word of the Bible. Accordingly, these people hold that every word of the Bible is of equal value with ever other word. Luther does not agree with this because he sees Christ as the heart and center of the Bible. As he said in his day, so he says now, "All Scriptures point to Christ alone. So we must cling to the pure Scriptures alone which teach nothing but Christ." Consequently, the Bible is evaluated according to the truth in Christ. All the books of the Bible are not of equal value. Esther and the Song of Solomon are inferior to Isaiah and Jeremiah; James and Revelation cannot compare with Romans and Galatians. The Word of God is Christ, and the Bible is the manger that holds Christ. And the significance of Christ is not in his teachings nor miracles but in his atoning death and resurrection.

With this understanding of the Bible as the Word of God in terms of the full and perfect revelation in Christ, Luther would oppose those who are trying to get Creationism taught in public schools. Fundamentalists, taking a literalist stance, claim that the Genesis account of creation is the one and only true explanation of creation. Luther says that the Bible does not pretend to be an authority in science but only in spiritual subjects. The spiritual essentials of the Genesis story concern who and why the universe was created. The method is relatively unimportant and is not necessary to accept for salvation. A Christian has a choice of accepting the science of Moses' day or the science of our day.

In contrast to literalism is today's allegorism. This is a reading into the Bible what is not really there. By the use of allegory, the

Bible is made to determine what the nations will do, when Armageddon will come, and the date of the end of the earth. This is illustrated in Lindsay's *The Late Great Planet Earth*. Luther would repudiate this handling of the Scriptures as he did the literalist interpretation. Luther was a Bible professor at Wittenberg University and earned his doctor's degree in Biblical studies. He urged us to examine the Scriptures critically, to delve into the authorship and occasion for writing in order to get to the original message of the writer. In other words, the Word of God is in the words of the Bible. Like miners we must dig into the words to get the deposit of gold, the truth of God in the Word.

On this issue in 1982 Luther spoke through a top leader of Jehovah's Witnesses, Raymond Franz, who for forty years devoted his life to his religion. With four others, he wrote the textbook on biblical interpretation for his sect. From his study of the Bible he began to question some of the teachings of Jehovah's Witnesses. He discovered that what his church taught was contrary to the Bible. He was taught that the Second Coming occurred in 1914 and that the end of the world would be in this generation. He began to see that the Bible sees the return of Christ as a future event. Further, he could not accept his church's denial of the deity of Christ. When he was put on trial, he paraphrased Luther's stand at Worms: "I assure you that if you will help me see from the Scriptures that the act of eating with Peter Gregerson is a sin, I will humbly repent of such sin before God."

Also, today Luther speaks to us about the Bible as the truth of the Gospel. This Gospel is simply stated, "Christ died for our sins . . . By grace are you saved through faith . . ." People have not changed in these past 500 years when it comes to getting salvation. Some still think, teach, and believe that salvation is for sale. In Luther's century, people tried to buy salvation by purchasing indulgences from John Tetzel. Today the Denver-based Church of World Peace will send by mail an indulgence for a thirty-five dollar fee which brings to you a Plenary Indulgence Certificate declaring that you have total forgiveness. How Luther would storm against this! In 1982 a special ABC-TV program, "Pray TV," called our attention to the begging of funds by the electronic church. Pat Robertson's 700 Club brings in $68 million annually. PTL has turned from "Praise the Lord" to "Pass the Loot." Luther stresses that we do not buy salvation but rather we are bought with a price — the holy and precious blood of Christ.

The Bible with the truth of the Gospel repudiates all modern efforts to save ourselves by our own efforts in terms of good works or character. Today people are the same in this as they were in Luther's day. In the sixteenth century people believed that they could earn merit to enter heaven by good works: prayers, pilgrimages, and payments to the church. In the twentieth century 4,371 lay church members were surveyed as to their beliefs. Forty-one percent stated that they considered the Gospel as "God's rules for right living." In his hymn, "Rock of Ages," Toplady has us sing the truth of the Gospel:

Not the labors of my hands
Can fulfill Thy law's demands.
Could my zeal no respite know,
Could my tears forever flow,
All for sin could not atone,
Thou must save and Thou alone.

A Word to the Church

The church, next to Jesus, meant everything to Luther. He loved the church so much that he gave his life to her cleansing and reforming so that she might be a fit bride for Christ. His high regard for the church can be seen in his statement: "Therefore he who wants to find Christ, must first find the church. Outside the church is no truth, no Christ, no salvation." For Luther, to be in Christ is to be in the church, for the body of Christ is the church. Because of his love and evaluation of the church, Luther — though dead like Abel — speaks to our church today.

Luther has something to say about the Roman Catholicism of our day. Indeed, he would rejoice and applaud the progress made since Vatican II. It took Catholicism 466 years to make the reforms he demanded in his day. He would enthusiastically approve the change in the language of the Mass from Latin to the vernacular, the present participation of the laity in the liturgy, the requirement of Biblical preaching at each Mass, and the collegiality with other Christian churches. Even in doctrine Luther would be amazed at the agreement expressed in the Lima, Peru, conference sponsored by the World Council of Churches in 1982, an agreement on the thorny subjects of baptism, eucharist, and ministry. On the other hand, Luther today would still be calling for further reforms. He would condemn some of the Catholic teachings as non-scriptural: the Immaculate Conception, the Blessed Assumption, the Infallability of the Pope, celibacy of the clergy, the prohibition of women priests, and the ban on birth control and abortion. If Luther would call for these reforms, would there be another Worms? Indeed, the Roman Church has a modern Luther in Hans Kung, who was relieved of his position as Roman Catholic theologian because he called for these reforms.

While Luther is calling for further reforms in the Roman Church, he is forthright in his condemnation of today's cults which are misleading millions of people into heresy. In his day, he condemned the heretics for their false teachings. He lambasted the Anabaptists and the Unitarians. Regretfully we must admit that Luther even agreed to sending sect leaders to death.

If Luther thought he had a problem with sects in his day, what would he do in our day with proliferation of cults that are drawing the faithful, especially young people, away from the church? Among the anti-Christian cults today are the Unification Church (Moonies), Scientology, Hare Krishna, Transcendental Meditation, Yoga, Astrology, Jehovah's Witnesses, Mormons, Christian Science, etc. Luther would be more than upset to see mainline churches decline while cults grow in great numbers. In no uncertain terms Luther would condemn these cults as twentieth century anti-Christs because of their non-biblical teachings. You can hear him thunder from the pulpit in showing that these cults are deadly wrong in teaching that the Bible is an insufficient revelation of divine truth, that there is a need for a leader who has a new revelation such as Moon's "Divine Principle." Luther would be horrified at the cult's claim that Jesus Christ is not sufficient for salvation. The cults teach that a new leader is necessary to fill the gaps in Jesus' life and ministry. Accordingly, Sun Moon of the Unification Church is considered to be the new Messiah, the Lord of the Second Advent. Furthermore the cults insist that the church is insufficient for the fellowship of true believers. They claim that only in their groups will you find true love, oneness, peace, and fellowship. For Luther and for us, these claims are totally false, they are contrary to God's Word, and therefore they are to be shunned, repudiated, and exterminated. But, not by force, Luther would insist, but by the proclamation of the Word of truth.

What about the twentieth century's electronic church? What would Luther say about it? If Luther were among us, he probably would seize radio and TV as a most wonderful way to proclaim the Word to the masses. In his day the marvel was the invention of printing, and he used the presses to scatter the Gospel. If it were not for the press, there may not have been a Reformation. No doubt, he would applaud the miraculous opportunity to preach the Gospel to hundreds of millions of people via radio and TV, and he would seize the opportunity.

Isn't this what the electronic church is doing? Yes, but Luther would object to the current electronic church. For one thing, he would say the church as a whole should assume the responsibility rather than certain individuals like Jim Bakker, Pat Robertson, Oral Roberts, Ron Hubbard, Jerry Falwell, and others. This results in a sectarian proclamation based upon an individual's concept of the Gospel without having the whole church to monitor, guide, and correct the proclamation. Why don't the main churches use radio and TV? Luther would say that this is one of the church's greatest faults, her sin of omission. The church has defaulted in its use of this modern miracle of communication and independent evangelists have filled the vacuum.

Not only who is using the media, but what is being done would concern Luther today. He would condemn the current practice of the electronic church to raise money by insistent and fervent appeals, by offering free gifts to get names and addresses for future solicitation. It is amazing that one TV evangelist receives $30 million each year while Pat Robertson goes even farther by getting $68 million. Luther would condemn the use of much of that money which is not spent on social service or missions but on the organization: fabulous salaries, mansions for the evangelists, extensive properties, and expensive equipment. The 700 Club boasts of a 387 acre headquarters with a $35 million complex and a $22 million studio. And a pittance for relieving human need and spreading the Word!

Probably Luther's main objection to the electronic church would be in the fact that the electronic church is only half a church. Millions are substituting the electronic church for the real church in the neighborhood. It is only a half church in the sense that it is impersonal. The preacher on the TV screen may be 1,000 miles away and he/she is not available for counseling nor help in time of need. When sickness, trouble, or death strikes, the electronic church is not on hand. Moreover, the electronic church is only half a church in view of the fact that worship is not a one-way street. Worship is not only listening to a spell-binder who puts on a performance or entertains. Worship calls for participation in praise, thanks, giving, and dedication of self.

In his day, Luther had much to say about the enthusiasts known as the "Schwarmerei." They were spiritual enthusiasts led by Carlstadt, Munzer, and the Zwickau Prophets. They rejected the liturgy, sacraments, religious art and music, the clergy, and infant baptism. They relied totally upon the spirit and believed the church was unnecessary and even of the devil. Luther was asked whether Thomas Munzer had the Holy Spirit. He replied, "Yes, he ate him up, feathers and all." Luther's position was that the external was needed as well as the internal, the body as well as the soul. He held to the position that the physical was not an impediment to the spirit.

Similarly, Luther would oppose the enthusiasts and spiritualists of our day who claim to be led by the Spirit without any regard for the external — church, Bible, clergy, or sacraments. In our day they claim to get direct directions from God through the Spirit for even the smallest concerns in life. They do not have an order of worship, for the Spirit will tell them what to do. There is no need to prepare a sermon, for at the time of the sermon the Spirit will tell the preacher what to say. The current enthusiasts claim to be filled with the Holy Spirit and able to perform miracles of healing and speaking in tongues. They insist they have had a second baptism of the Spirit and received the Spirit in some sudden, spectacular, emotional experience. In contrast, Luther says that the Spirit does not come nor work in this totally internal way but comes and works regularly through the proper channels of Word and Sacraments. In fact, the Spirit is always connected with the Word, for he said, "God will not give his Spirit apart from the external Word."

Church and State: Who Rules?

Luther had to confront not only the powerful Roman Church but also the mighty Holy Roman Empire under the emperor, Charles V. He was not only excommunicated by the Church but was outlawed by the State for his religious convictions. This was a definite violation of the separation of church and state. Because of this, Luther from the time of Worms in 1517 lived in constant fear of arrest as a heretic. If it had not been for his friendly prince, Frederick the Wise, he would have been burned as a heretic under the auspices of the state and church.

The separation of church and state was the practical implication of Luther's theology, based on Scripture, that God ruled with two hands. God has two kingdoms. With one hand he rules the kingdom of justice through the state and with the other he rules the kingdom of grace through the church. These hands must never join nor be crossed over each other. Church and state are divinely meant to be separate. This is a problem for all generations, for as long as church and state exist side by side.

Luther would say to us today that the state has no right to use the church for its own purposes. Luther opposed the attempts of the state to use the church to make changes. There was a group of German nationalists led by Ulrich von Hutten and Franz von Sickingen, who espoused Luther's cause and wanted to turn the Reformation into a national movement to free Germany from the Pope and Charles V. They had their own army and volunteered to protect Luther from both the church and empire. Luther refused their offer of aid and even at a time when his life was threatened, he did not believe that the kingdom was established by force of arms but only by the Word.

In similar manner, the peasants of Germany saw in Luther their champion for better economic conditions. At first Luther sympathized with the plight of the peasants' poverty. They rallied around Luther and supported his opposition to Rome as a part of their program to get out of poverty. When the peasants turned to rebellion — murder, rape, fire, torture — he turned against them and called upon the princes to squash the revolution with arms. He refused to make the Gospel a holy war for better economic and social conditions.

In our day, the state attempts to use the church to carry out its principles. A case in point is the Bob Jones University which was threatened with the withdrawal of non-tax status because of its racial policies. If the state can withdraw tax benefits from a church or church-related institution, it is using force to make the church abide by its principles and policies. If it is the racial issue this time, what could the state do about other teachings of the church?

It is just as dangerous and unscriptural for the church to use the state as a means to promote her cause. Luther would say that the church has no right to use the state. This was the case at the Diet of Worms. The church called upon the state under Emperor Charles V to carry out its decree of excommunication. Because of friendly princes, the state was unable to enforce its ban on Luther.

In our times Luther would condemn any political theocracy where religious leaders ruled the state. We have a case of this violation of church and state in Iran where Islamic Fundamentalists under Ayatollah Khomeini have executed over the past three years 4,000 political opponents and kept American hostages for 444 days. In the name of religion, thousands have been tortured to death.

Luther was against those who wanted the Reformation to

dictate laws and morality to the state, to punish heretics, and to engage in holy wars. It is not right nor Christian for a minority's morality to be imposed upon the majority by legal force. We face this issue in our day. A segment of today's church calls upon the state to pass laws prohibiting abortion. Fundamentalists in Moral Majority are working to have the state permit prayer in public schools. If certain politicians do not vote according to their religious principles, they are black-balled and are put up for defeat in the next election. The church in terms of Don Wildmon and his Coalition for Better Television threatens to use a boycott of TV sponsors who have shows that do not properly depict Christian values.

Force is not the method for social change, according to Luther. Nothing good is accomplished by force. The power of social improvement is the Word of God. Only the Word has the power to change the hearts of people to effect change. When the Knights of Germany offered military assistance in establishing the Reformation, Luther wrote to Spalatin, "I am not willing to fight for the gospel with bloodshed. The world is conquered by the Word, and by the Word the church is served and rebuilt." Luther would say to us in these days of Moral Majority, Fundamentalism, and censorship, preach and teach the Word, and let the Word bring a change in society. It is not right to impose by force a religion or a morality on an unwilling minority or majority. Let the state be the state as the minister of God using the sword of justice, and let the church be the church in its use of the sword of the Spirit, the Word of God.

Oh, if Luther were here today to lead and speak to us about our moral and spiritual problems! There would be a new Reformation where truth would abide and sinners saved. On this 500th birthday celebration let Luther, like Abel, speak to you personally about salvation through grace alone, about the true nature of the church, and about your participation in church and state. You will find that he speaks to you the truth of God's Word, and that truth can make you free.

I Love Luther

"This I command you, to love one another." (John 15:17)
That disciple whom Jesus loved said to Peter, "It is the Lord."
(John 21:7.)

The TV show, "I Love Lucy," has been popular for years. Why love only Lucy? Why not Mary and Barbara and Jane? According to Jesus, we are to love everyone, even our enemies: "This I command you, to love one another." Even if we did love each other, there would be one whom we would love more. When we were children, (you remember, don't you?) we played the game of drop the handkerchief. We joined hands in a circle and sang, "Ring around the rosies," while one with a handkerchief went around the outside of the circle and dropped the handkerchief at the feet of the person he/she loved the best.

This is a normal fact of life. Even Jesus had a special love for John. In the last three chapters of John's Gospel, John is referred to four times as "the disciple whom Jesus loved." Didn't Jesus love each of his Disciples? Of course, he did but obviously there is one he loved the best.

That is the case with me and Luther. On this 500th anniversary of Martin Luther's birth, I want to testify that "I love Luther." Of course, I love other great Christian leaders such as Paul, Augustine, Calvin, Knox, John Wesley, Phillips Brooks, and Peter Marshall, but above all these I love Luther. On this occasion when we renew our acquaintance with Luther, I submit to you that he is worthy to be loved by everyone. Maybe he is not the one you love best, as I do, but at least you cannot help but love him for what he was and did for the kingdom of God, a work that lasts to this day. If Jesus were on earth today and called Luther as one of the Twelve, perhaps Luther would have been identified as "the disciple whom Jesus loved." You, too, will love Luther when you get to know him, and the better you know him, the more you will love him.

A Lovable Man

With me you will love Luther because of his humanness. His being a real person makes him lovable. He is real and genuine as a human being. He began life as a "nothing." His parents were peasants; his father worked in the mines. Luther as a child was so poor that he had to take to the streets to beg and sing. His father dreamed that his son would one day be a lawyer, but soon after graduating from Erfurt University, Luther took a vow of poverty as an Augustinian monk. Yet, later he became a learned professor of Bible and reformed the church. From 1517 to 1546 Luther was in the spotlight of the world's attention as the rediscoverer of the Gospel. Whether he was on the bottom or the top rung of life's ladder, he was always a frank, real, earthy, blustery, and often, by today's standards, crude person. He was a man among men.

One of the aspects of his humanity that makes you love him is his humility. Though he turned his religious world right side up by his preaching, teaching, and writing, he never, ever, boasted of his ability or his accomplishments. He had the grace to see himself as a "lost and condemned creature," one "without any merit or worthiness." He saw himself as an instrument of God and used by God for his glory. It is like a concert pianist seated at a grand piano. The Steinway is a marvelous instrument. The tone is beautiful. The master-pianist does his very best to play the instrument. If the piano were broken or out of tune, the best artist could not produce the best music. When the concert is over, the audience does not come up and admire the Steinway or rave about its mechanical perfection or the tone quality. No, the audience applauds and shouts "Bravo" to the master-pianist, and not a single word or glance is given to the piano. So it was with Luther. He took no credit for what music of God he played; he was only an instrument in God's hands. The Master was given the glory. Thus Luther said, "I ask that men make no reference to my name and call themselves not Lutherans but Christians." In his humility he said, "I did nothing; the Word did everything." St. Paul wrote, "If any one is in Christ, he is a new creation." Luther reminds us that God creates out of nothing. If we are to be something, we must first be nothing.

Luther's humanness is seen also in his relations with others. He loved common, ordinary people even though he was a brilliant doctor of theology and hero of the Reformation. At times he could be rough, brash, and crude, but he could also be tender, sweet, and soft. In his sermons he addressed the servants and peasants rather than the professors and students of the university. When his barber asked him how to pray, Luther wrote an explanation entitled, "Master Peter the Barber: A Simple Way to Pray." In his marriage relationship there was tenderness and love, even though he married, as he explained it, "to spite the Papacy, please his father, and to confirm his teachings." At a meal, his wife, Katie, asked him, "Why don't you stop talking and start eating?" He replied, "I wish women would say the Lord's Prayer before opening their mouths!" With his children, he was a caring and loving father. When on trips, he would occasionally write letters to his sons in terms of childhood concerns and language. When his daughter died, Luther was overcome with grief, but admitted that heaven was a far better place for her.

Though Luther was a monk in armor, and fiercely fought church and state in defense of the Gospel, he was human enough at times to be weak and mistaken. Throughout his life, he suffered "Anfechtungen" — despondency, despair, and discouragement. One time he confessed, "For more than a week I was close to the gates of death and hell." During one of the depression seizures, Katie persuaded Luther to take a walk. While he was gone, she put on black mourning clothes. When he returned and saw her in black, he asked, "Who died that you are dressed in black?" She explained, "God died." "What do you mean, 'God died'? You know God cannot die." In response Katie said, "Is that so? I thought God died because you were so despondent."

Like all of us, Luther was not perfect. He acted and reacted like a typical human being. One of his mistakes was his over-reaction to the Peasants' War. Repudiating force as a means of social reform, Luther called upon the princes to slay the peasants who revolted and went on a rampage. When he was disappointed that Jews did not accept the newfound gospel, he was guilty of anti-Semitic writings and expressions. Near the close of his life, he advised bigamy as a solution to a prince's miserable marriage. He, as well as we, had reason to exclaim, "Oh, my sins, my sins!" With a realization of our human tendency to sin, more than ever are we grateful for a merciful God who gave his Son as a sacrifice for our sins that we might be forgiven and go to heaven.

A Christ Man

If you love Christ, you have to love Luther, for he was a Christ-conscious man, a Christ-centered man, a Christ-saturated man. He lived, fought, and died for the truth of the gospel. And the gospel is the good news that Jesus is the human-divine Son of God who was enfleshed in Jesus to reveal the truth of God and to redeem humanity. In Christ was the perfect manifestation of the grade which saves through faith. For Luther, Christ was all-in-all and he was out-and-out for Christ. The Reformation did not really begin with Luther's nailing the 95 Theses on the castle church door on October 31, 1517, but began when Luther discovered the righteousness of God in Christ.

For Luther, Christ is the way to God, the only way. He really believed Jesus' words, "I am the way." With certainty and conviction, Luther said, "He will not find God outside of Christ." That is a daring and revolutionary statement in these modern days of pluralism which holds that there are many valid ways to God and heaven. According to some modern thinkers, one does not have to be a Christian to know or get to God. Frankly Luther said, "He who doesn't believe in Christ cannot be saved." This is an embarrassing statement for liberals and modernists who place Jesus as just one of the prophets. For the Scriptures and for Luther, Jesus saves. This means that Christ by the cross opened the way to God, and sinners, covered by the righteousness of Christ, are received into God's presence. In all of the Christian explanations and descriptions of the significance of Christ, no finer nor more comprehensive statement on Christ has been written than Luther's explanation of the second article of the Apostles' Creed:

> *I believe that Jesus Christ, true God, begotten of the Father from eternity, and also true man, born of the Virgin Mary, is my Lord; who has redeemed me, a lost and condemned creature, secured and delivered me from all sins, from death, and from the power of the devil, not with silver and gold, but with His holy and precious blood, and with His innocent sufferings and death; in order that I might be His own, live under Him in His kingdom, and serve Him in everlasting righteousness, innocence, and blessedness; even as He is risen from the dead, and lives and reigns to all eternity. This is most certainly true.*

Since Jesus is the one and only way to God, we have reason to engage in evangelism and missions to reach all people with the good news of redemption and release for sin-bound people with or without a religion. The tragedy of our times is that in an average congregation, 95 percent of the members make no effort to witness for Christ in the hope of gaining non-Christians as believers in Christ and members of the church. In these times of inflation, mainline churches are reducing the number and support of missionaries overseas. How can people believe in Christ if they are not told the Word?

In addition, for Luther, Christ is the whole truth of God. Jesus also said, "I am the truth." Christ is the Word incarnate. The Word is truth and Jesus is the personification of God's truth. To know Jesus, therefore, is to know the truth. In John's gospel, Jesus says, "If you continue in my word, you are truly my disciples, and you will know the truth . . ." He is not a partial truth but the final and perfect truth of God. In former times God spoke through the prophets, but in Christ God spoke his final Word. As Jesus said about himself, "He that hath seen me hath seen the Father."

If we understand and accept this, there is no reason for sects or cults who claim to have truth beyond the Scriptures. There is no need of a Book of Mormon, nor "Science and Health: A Key to the Scriptures," nor a "Divine Principle." Barth, Bonhoeffer, Bultmann, Tillich, Kirkegaard, and Niebuhr cannot add to the truth of Christ; at best they can only help us understand the perfect revelation in Christ. There is enough truth in Christ to give you all you need to know about God, life, man, and salvation.

Luther saw the Bible as the truth of the Word, the incarnate Word, Christ. The Bible is the manger and the swaddling cloths for the Christ. He is the center and heart of the Bible. He is the key to understanding and interpreting the Scriptures. Thus, the Bible is evaluated by Christ, and what falls short of his teachings and spirit is unacceptable to us Christians. This saves us from literalists who find themselves in all kinds of trouble in interpreting and applying the Bible to modern conditions. Seeing Christ as the Word, we are saved from legalism and fundamentalism while still being true to the Scriptures. In Christ we are free to live by the spirit and not by the letter of the Law. And for this wonderful and liberating approach to the Bible, we can thank Luther.

For Luther, Christ is preeminent in giving life. Jesus said he was life and that he came to give abundant life. God is life and as the Son of God, Christ is life and gives life to all believers. He who is in Christ has life which is eternal. This means that each person to have life must have a personal experience with Christ. It is not enough to know about Jesus but to know him in a personal and intimate way. Once Luther wrote, "It is not enough that you say Luther, Peter, Paul have said so, but you must experience Christ himself in your conscience . . ." Pointing to his heart Luther said, "If you would knock on the door of my heart and ask, 'Who lives here?' I would not say, 'Martin Luther lives here.' I would say, 'Jesus Christ lives here.' " If one would knock on the door of your heart, would you be able to say, "Jesus Christ lives here"?

A Brave Man

I love Luther because he was a man of faith. When you know of his faith, you, too, will love him, for his faith is inspiring and contagious.

Luther had faith in the saving power of the gospel. Salvation was not for sale by buying indulgences. Getting right with God was not in obeying the laws of the church. Not even doing good or performing religious acts of devotion such as prayers, masses, or pilgrimages, could earn your acceptance by God. Luther so believed in faith for salvation that in translating the Bible, he added the word, "alone" when the text said we are justified by grace through faith. Faith is the agent of accepting the grace of God in Christ the Savior. Even before we repent and believe, God loves us and wishes to reconcile us for Jesus' sake. Faith is not a work that merits forgiveness. Faith presupposes the goodness and mercy of God, who long before we even knew of God and ourselves as sinners, took the initiative to save us by sending Christ. Faith trusts God's mercy and makes the gift of acceptance a personal possession. The gospel is the absolute truth, and Luther believed it and staked his life on it. When excluded from the church, he kept this faith and was not scared of being condemned. When banned by the empire, he kept the faith even if it meant death at the stake. His example makes us wonder if our faith is strong enough to pay any price of personal loss for the Gospel.

His faith was also in the power of God's Word. Luther really believed that the Word could change and transform both individual and corporate life. In "A Mighty Fortress" Luther has us sing, "One little word shall fell him." One little word of the Bible, according to Luther, has power to overcome Satan! What power! What faith! Since the Word had the power, Luther did not believe in the use of force to overcome social, religious, or political evils. He would say that all we need do is to proclaim fearlessly the Word, and God will fight the battle for us. Referring to overcoming the Pope, he said, "He must be exterminated by the Word and by prayer."

The reason for the Word's power is the presence of the Holy Spirit in the Word. Word and Spirit, for Luther, are inseparable.

The Spirit comes to us through the channel of the Word in Scripture. Thus, the Word is to be preached, and this means that biblical preaching alone is acceptable. The Word needs to be read by every Christian, and thus Luther translated the Bible into the language of the people that they might benefit from the power of the Word. Word, Bible, Spirit, and power are one. Is this not reason enough to once more get back to the Bible as the answer to our problems?

Moreover, Luther had faith in God's providence. He really believed that God and his Word could be trusted. He believed in the promises of God and by faith laid hold of them. When he and his friends burned the papal announcement (bull) that he was excommunicated, he did not recant in fearful submission but in calm faith threw the "bull" into the fire in defiance of the false teachings of the church. When he was summoned for trial at Worms, Luther said that if there were as many devils in Worms as tiles on the roofs, he would still come and make his confession of faith in the truth of the Gospel. Faith gave him heroic courage. When radicals threatened to undo the Reformation, voluntarily he came out of hiding in the Wartburg castle to go back to Wittenberg to take over the reform movement. This was his chief act of courage because he subjected himself to arrest and death as a heretic. When Luther's protector, Frederick the Wise, was said to be withdrawing his support, a friend asked Luther, "If your prince withdraws his support, where will you be?" Luther replied, "Right where I have always been — on the arms of the everlasting God." His was a faith that was faithful unto death. On his deathbed, he was asked, "Dear Doctor, with you is the Lord Christ. Do you intend to continue hanging on to him?" From the heart, he said his last word: "YES." As we consider Luther's faith, we want to sing:

Faith of our fathers, holy faith,
We will be true to thee till death.

In obedience to Christ, we are to love all people, but following Jesus' example, there is one human we may love more than others. In my case and hopefully in yours, I love Luther. How could you not love one who loved Christ supremely and one who proclaimed that love faithfully and fearlessly?

The Struggle for Faith

"I believe; help my unbelief." (Mark 9:24)

On this 500th anniversary of Luther's birth or at any other time, no one can deny that Luther was a giant of faith. His great faith made him great. By his faith he overcame the twin powers of state and church. By means of his faith the church was renewed and reformed. The Gospel was rediscovered and believers regained their religious freedom to think, to believe, to worship, and to live according to their enlightened consciences. If Jesus were on earth at the time of Luther, he probably would have said to Luther as he said to the Syrophoenician woman who persisted in pleading for her demon-possessed daughter, "O woman (man), great is your faith." Similarly, Jesus probably would have remarked about Luther's faith as he did about the Centurion's: "Not even in Israel (Germany) have I found such faith."

As we review Luther's faith, we exclaim, "Oh, for a faith like that!" We covet such a faith, but we realize we are more like the epileptic's father at the foot of Mt. Transfiguration who said to Jesus, "I believe; help my unbelief." We believe to some extent but we have miles to go before we have a faith as we want to have. How does one get a great faith like Luther's? Is it a divine gift or it it a human achievement? Does faith come suddenly or gradually?

A Faith Worth the Struggle

To get our answers we examine Luther's faith. First of all, we see that he had the kind of faith that was worth the struggle. With the text Luther could say, "I believe." He had faith in the providence of God. In his *Small Catechism* Luther elaborated on his faith in God the Father: "I believe that God has created me and all that exists . . . that he daily provides me abundantly with all the necessities of life, protects me from all danger, and preserves and guards me against all evil . . ." He was sure that God cares, loves, and protects his children. When Luther was told that his protector, Frederick the Wise, might withdraw his support, he was asked, "Then where will you be, Martin?" "Right where," he replied, "I have always been — on the arms of the everlasting God."

With this faith, he was confident that God would take care of him even if all his enemies came together to attack him. One of his favorite Psalms was the 46th — "God is our refuge and strength, a very present help in trouble. Therefore we will not fear though the earth be removed . . . Be still and know that I am God." This bold confidence was expressed in his hymn, A Mighty Fortress:

> And though this world, with devils filled,
> Should threaten to undo us;
> We will not fear, for God hath willed
> His truth to triumph through us . . .

Luther literally put his life in God's hands. When radicals caused chaos in Wittenberg while he was in the Wartburg castle, he decided to return and straighten things out. If he did so, he was subject to immediate arrest and execution as a heretic. Upon leaving the castle, he wrote to Frederick the Wise, "I am coming home. I am not asking you to protect me. If I thought you would protect me with the sword, I would not come."

His faith, moreover, was a faith in the Savior, Son of God. Here was the heart of his faith which prompted his break with Roman Catholicism. Jesus died for our sins. He paid the price for our sins on the cross and fulfilled the law in our behalf. Because of this, sinners who accept him are acceptable to God. Here is the fulness of grace by which alone we are saved. His faith in Christ is summed up in his Small Catechism: "I believe that Jesus Christ, true God, begotten of the Father from eternity, and also true man, born of the Virgin Mary, is my Lord; who redeemed me, a lost and condemned creature, secured and delivered me from all sins, from death, and from the power of the devil, not with silver and gold, but with His holy and precious blood, and with His innocent sufferings and death . . ."

Faith in Christ makes our redemption a personal reality and possession. As Paul Tillich said, by faith we accept our acceptance. Having been released from the bondage of ourselves with our sins, we express gratitude by worship, witness, service, and obedience to God's will.

In addition, Luther's faith was in the Holy Spirit and his power. The Spirit is in the believer. Since the Spirit is God, the Spirit gives to the believer the very power of God. In accord with the Scriptures Luther held that the Spirit was in, with, and under the Word recorded in the Bible. There is power in the Word of God, because God's Spirit is in it. The Word has the power to call people to faith, to transform a sinner into a saint, and change society for the better. Consequently, Luther did not believe in using external force to make believers nor to correct social, political or economic evils. It was enough to teach and preach the Word, and then in due time the Word will effect changes. Unlike Szingli, the Reformed leader, Luther refused to take up arms in defense of the Gospel. He refused the armed protection of the German nationalists, Hutten and Sickingen. In one of his sermons Luther explained, "I opposed indulgences and all the papists, but never with force. I simply taught, preached, and wrote God's Word. Otherwise I did nothing. And while I slept or drank Wittenberg beer with my friends, Philip and Amsdorf, the Word so greatly weakened the papacy that no prince nor emperor ever afflicted such losses upon it. I did nothing; the Word did everything." In our day with manifold social problems, Luther would still call upon the church to change society by faithfully proclaiming the Word in sermon and sacrament.

A Struggle to Get Faith

This wonderful faith of Luther did not come easily nor suddenly. His faith came out of great tribulation. His experience is a pattern for us in getting faith. Like the Father of the epileptic, we know our faith is far from being great. We come to Jesus with the prayer, "Help my unbelief." Luther had to struggle with his unbelief. To get faith he had to go through an agony of soul.

It was a struggle for Luther and is a struggle for us to get faith in a gracious God. In his childhood and youth, his church and society gave him a God of justice and wrath. There was fear of God's judgment upon sinners. The atmosphere was one of demons, witchcraft, and superstition. Luther had a tough childhood with extreme severity and discipline. His family's extreme poverty made him beg for food by singing outside affluent homes. For stealing a nut, his mother whipped him until the blood flowed. Because of his father's severe beatings, one time he ran away from home. Luther tells of being caned twelve times in one morning by his school teacher for no reason at all.

Being scared to death of a vengeful God, Luther had a life-changing experience while returning to the Unviversity of Erfurt where he was studying to please his father to be a lawyer. Lightning struck so close that he was knocked to the ground. He prayed, "St. Anne, help me. I will become a monk." Accordingly, he entered an Augustinian monastery in Erfurt. His father was infuriated at his decision. Luther escaped to monkhood in order to be saved from God's wrath and to earn entrance to heaven.

His struggle to have faith in a gracious God was seen when he was ordained a priest and offered his first mass. He was terror-stricken to stand at the altar in the very presence of a holy and righteous God. It took all his will power to offer the bread and wine, the very literal body and blood of Christ, as a sacrifice for sins. His hands trembled, his voice cracked, his knees wobbled. He was overcome with the experience of coming so close to a God of justice and holiness.

To find a God full of compassion, mercy, and understanding was a struggle. Would that we today had more respect and reverence for God and his house! We treat sacred things so lightly and casually as though God was not a God of glory and power and majesty.

Moreover, it was a struggle for Luther and is for us, too, to get faith in the Gospel. In his day, a person worked his/her way into the good graces of God by doing good works as prescribed by the church: penance, confession, masses, prayers, alms, pilgrimages. For the first time he began to doubt the salvation system of his church. When in Rome representing his monastic order, he climbed the sacred stairs in front of St. John Lateran Church on his hands and knees with an "Our Father" said on each step (twenty-eight in all). When he reached the top, he asked, "Who knows whether it is so?"

The struggle to get faith in the Gospel continued in the monastery. He obeyed all the laws and performed all the denials required and more so. In winter he afflicted his body by lying naked on the cold floor of his cell. He fasted until he fainted for lack of food. Since only confessed sin could be forgiven, he confessed his sins for six hours on a stretch. Once he said, "If ever a man could get to heaven through monkery, that man would be me." There was a time when Luther actually hated God and Paul. Luther confessed, "I hated Paul with all my heart when I read that the righteousness of God is revealed in the Gospel." He felt that God was unjust and unfair to demand a righteousness he could not attain by his own efforts. He was angry with God for asking the impossible and then condemning a sinner for not reaching moral perfection. Do we also not say that God asks too much of us? Do we not also get mad at God for allowing hardships and crises to come to us? What kind of God is he anyway? If Luther were living today, he would probably picket the church, carrying a placard, "Unfair to sinners." In John Osborne's *Luther*, Luther says, "It's just this. All I can feel, all I can feel is God's hatred." A fellow monk replies, "You're a fool.

You're really a fool. God isn't angry with you. It's you who are angry with him." Both Luther and we must struggle with this anger against God.

In addition, Luther had to struggle through the false teachings of his church, through salvation by works, through legalism and humanism to get to the truth of the Gospel where he found a gracious God and salvation by grace alone through faith alone. Fortunately, Luther was ordered to earn a doctor's degree in biblical studies and then was appointed professor of Bible at Wittenberg University. This made him search the Scriptures where he discovered the truth about God and our salvation. He found the truth in Romans and Galatians where Paul enunciated justification by faith. When he discovered the truth while preparing his Bible lectures, he found the Gospel. He explained how he felt: "I felt myself to be reborn and to have gone through open doors into paradise."

The Bible was the source of his new faith, the faith that changed the church and brought life and liberty to millions upon millions over the past 500 years. The Bible was the infallible Word of God. Upon it he based his teaching and his work of reformation. His devotion to the Word was expressed in another of his hymns:

Lord, keep us steadfast in thy Word.
Curb those who fain by craft or sword
Would wrest the kingdom from thy Son,
And set at naught all he has done.

Struggle to Keep the Faith

It is one thing to have faith and it is another to keep it. Every Christian, including Luther, has to struggle to keep the faith and not only to keep it but to let it grow. The fact is that faith, unlike grace, can diminish and can be lost. The resurrected Christ said, "Be faithful unto death, and I will give you the crown of life."

Like us, Luther had to struggle against temptation to keep his evangelical faith. Satan was very real to him and he felt the tempter's power. It seems that the closer one is to God, the greater is the temptation. Satan often tempted Jesus. There is a legend that when Luther was translating the Bible while in the Wartburg, the devil became so real that Luther threw his ink well at him. To this day, tourists are shown the broken plaster where the ink well supposedly hit the wall. Indeed, Luther's struggle against temptation was successful. According to legend, one night Luther became aware of a terrifying, cold, sinister presence in his room. He turned over and saw the devil sitting in a corner of the room. He said, "Oh, it's you!" Then Luther turned over and went to sleep. Luther explained. "The devil is a toothless bulldog. He looks fierce, but for the Christian he has no bite."

For years Luther had to struggle to keep his faith because of discouragement and depression. These attacks were known as "Anfechtungen." He explained the depth to which he could go: "For more than a week I was close to the gates of death and hell. I trembled in all my members. Christ was wholly lost. I was shaken by desperation and blasphemy of God." One time his wife, Katharine von Bora, shocked him out of his depression. When Luther went for a walk, she dressed in black mourning clothes. When he returned, he anxiously asked, "Who died?" She said sadly, "God died." Luther protested, "That is not true. You know God cannot die." "Well", she explained, "I thought he must have died because you were so depressed."

How can we keep the faith God gave us through the Word? How did Luther keep his faith? Whenever he doubted his salvation, he referred to his baptism. He said he would crawl on his hands and knees to the font and there be reminded that at this place God adopted him as his child. It was there that God made a covenant of salvation with us, and God never breaks his promises. At baptism the grace of God is experienced, sins washed away, and a new creature is born of the Spirit. Luther said, "I have been baptized and I have the Word, and I have no doubt about my salvation as long as I continue to cling to the Word."

Another way, according to Luther, is to rely upon God's promises in the Bible and not upon personal feelings. Our feelings are emotional and they come and go. If we base our faith on feelings, the day will come when we no longer feel that we are God's people. To have assurance that we are God's people, that we have been forgiven, and that we are destined to heaven, we need to rely on the promises of God by faith. Luther explained, "If you will not believe that the Word is worth more than all you see or feel, then reason has blinded faith. I do not feel Christ is risen, but the Word affirms it. So one must not be guided by one's feelings but by his Word."

To keep the faith, have fellowship with believers. When doubts and discouragement threatened his faith, Luther was helped by his friends. He enjoyed talking over his Wittenberg beer and at his table there was always a group of professors, students, and family. Out of these conversations came his famous *Table Talk*. Faith is contagious. When we need to be bolstered and refreshed in faith, we need to get in fellowship with other Christians. In numbers there is safety. A public school teacher announced plans to take her seventh graders to New York City to see the sights and visit educational centers. One mother was concerned that one adult could not manage a class of children in a big city. She was reluctant to let her son go. After some pleading she let him go with his class to the big city. When he returned, his mother asked some questions. "Did they have any problems?" "No." "Did the teacher have any assistants?" "No." "Did the teacher have any special instructions for you?" The boy simply said, "All she told us was to hold on to the rope." To keep the group together that no one would be lost, she had them hold on to a rope as they crossed crowded streets and went from place to place. The church is our rope of fellowship. As long as we hold on to the rope, we will keep our faith.

In John Osborne's *Luther*, Cajetan says to Luther, "I've read some of your sermons on faith. Do you know all they say to me?" Luther replies, "No." Cajetan continues: "They say, I am a man struggling for certainty, struggling insanely like a man in a fit, an animal trapped to the bone with doubt." For us, too, faith is a struggle, a struggle to get and keep it. When Luther was on his death bed, two of his friends asked him, "Dear Doctor, with you is the Lord Christ. Do you intend to continue hanging on to him?" From his heart, Luther uttered his last word, "Yes." He was faithful to faith till death in spite of a long-life struggle to get and keep faith. With God's help and with Luther's example to inspire us, we, too, can be steadfast in our struggle to the very end of life. To such Jesus promises, "I will give you the crown of life."

Here We Stand

So then, brethern, stand firm and hold to the traditions . . . (2 Thessalonians 2:15)

When the right words are spoken at the right time and at the right place they sometimes become immortal. This was true in the revolutionary period when Patrick Henry cried out, "Give me liberty or give me death!" Those words aroused the states to fight for independence. During the Civil War when the nation was torn in two, a thin, tall man spoke at the dedication of a cemetery in Gettysburg and concluded his brief address with the immortal words: "This government of the people, by the people, and for the people shall not perish from the earth." These words still live as a reminder to keep a united democracy. During the second World War the allies were at a low ebb of discouragement. A short, rotund man gave a rousing speech in which was the phrase, "Blood, sweat, and tears." These words sparked the West to pay the price to defeat totalitarianism.

In the field of religion there were no more famous words than those spoken by a German peasant, an Augustinian monk. For his teaching and preaching against the false teachings and immoral practices of his church, he was excommunicated by Rome and now he was called to a Diet held in Worms, Germany in 1521, to be tried whether or not he should be banned by the empire. You must see the situation. The hall was crowded with prelates of the church and princes from the realm. They were assembled in all their glorious robes and heraldry. There was a table in the center on which there were a number of books. A prosecutor by the name of Eck asked this monk, Martin Luther, whether he would recant what he wrote in his books. He simply said that if he could be shown that his writings were contrary to Scripture, he himself would burn the books, but if not, then his conscience was bound to the Word of God. Then came the immortal words, "Here I stand. I cannot do otherwise. God help me." The statement electrified the assembly and the world admired this new hero of the faith, the father of Protestant Reformation.

Luther was doing nothing other than following the guidance of St. Paul. He was doing what Paul told his people in

Thessalonica to do: "stand firm and hold to the traditions." Likewise, Paul writing to the Ephesians told his people to put on the armor of God and having done all to stand. Similarly he wrote to the Galatians, "Stand fast in the liberty wherewith Christ has made you free." There comes a time when true Christians must take a stand. If we are true followers of Luther, we will follow his example by saying, "Here we stand." How badly that is needed in our day! We face ideological differences, theological confusion, and changing values. Everything we thought was nailed down has come loose and the only thing certain in our times is uncertainty. The time has come to say, "Here we stand." And not only to say it, but to do it!

Stand Against It

What does it mean to stand! One thing it means is to stand against all manner of evil and falsehood. The forces of righteousness and truth must stand against the bitter enemies of goodness and faith. Does today's Christian stand against anything, or is it characteristic of him to roll with the punches and to tolerate whatever comes down the road? Are we guilty of compromising with the world rather than fighting it? Are we opposed to what is taking place in the world? In recent months it has been reported that there is an increase in church attendance and some think religion is going to have another surge forward, but at the same time crime is increasing far more rapidly than church membership. Is this not an ironical paradox and inconsistency? If Christians are truly Christians, should there not be a rise in morality? Some of us may be like the man about whom the late Bishop Arthur J. Moore told. The man had been absent from the community for some years. When he came back he gave this testimony to a Wednesday night prayer meeting. He confessed, "I admit I haven't been a very good person. I got drunk many times. I have had affairs with women. I have cursed and sworn. I spent a lot of time in jail. But I want to tell you that through it all I never lost my religion."

The time is here when we should take a stand against all that is un-Christian in society and fight against every form of wickedness with all our might. Did you hear how the famous general of the Civil War got the name "Stonewall Jackson?" The Confederate army was in retreat. As the soldiers were falling back, one saw Jackson not budging an inch. A soldier cried to his comrades, "Look at Jackson standing there like a stone wall." Since that time he was known as Stonewall Jackson. While the hordes of godlessness keep coming at us, each of us could well be like a stone wall, refusing to yield to the pressure of wickedness. This is what Lincoln did when early in his life he watched a black family being sold, the husband to one owner and the wife to another who lived far from each other. He determined at that time that this cruel separation of a family by slavery had to be eradicated. In his day Luther took a stand against evil teachings and practices. He stood against buying your way into heaven by the purchase of indulgences. He was against the church's dispensation of grace through an automatic reception of the sacraments. Luther fought against the church's placing tradition above the authority of the Word.

But now it is 462 years later. Would Luther be against the same things? No, because those evils, thankfully, are no longer issues. If Luther were alive today, he would be against other equally serious evils that exist in our society. He would have us stand against the secularism of our day. More and more our society is getting secularized. Secularism is that movement that is sucking the spirituality out of society. God is ignored as being unimportant. God is left out of our thinking and living. You can see the effects of secularism on our Sunday, once a holy day for rest and religion. Now Sunday is just another day, a day for shopping, work, recreation, and travel. Already in October Christmas decorations are being put up and the commercialization of Christmas, starts. Santa has replaced the Christ-child. Similarly, secularization has turned Easter from the glorious resurrection account to a myth about an Easter bunny.

We need to take a stand against the humanism of our day. This is the idea that it is great to be a human. Each person is a value in himself, the highest value of life. Man is in the center of things and his theme song is, "Glory to man in the highest!" One of the current best-selling books is entitled *Looking out for #1*. We have turned around the saying of the Prodigal Son to say, "Father, you have sinned and are no more worthy to be called my father." The disease of today is narcissism. Self is at the center of our existence. The other day we saw a young woman with a T-shirt having the message: "I am his for he deserves the best." This pride and self-centeredness is what we as Christians fight against.

Christians fight also against immorality in our day. Wickedness has become a way of life. To do evil is considered routine. Nobody raises an eyebrow. No one is embarrassed. No one raises the question whether it is ethical. We all know we have corruption in politics, crime on the streets, and perversity in sex. A certain employer was interviewing candidates for an open position. When one man came for his interview, he was asked, "What do two and two make?" He quickly answered, "Four." Sorry, he was not acceptable. Another man came in and he was asked the same question. The candidate leaned over the desk and in a whisper asked, "How much do you want it to make?" He got the job! Unless Christians stand against the immorality of our day, there is no hope for a better America. We must fight against crime. Evil must be curtailed and eradicated from our society. Laws will not do it because laws are always broken. Jails will not reform criminals. A recent report tells us that our jails are packed and can take no more, and thus the situation threatens our penal system because we have no place to put the offenders. The real answer is obedience to God and faith in Christ. We fight against all who are against God and his will.

Stand for It

Here we stand. We know now what we need to stand against, but what are we standing for? It is not enough to be negative; we are to be positive in our approach and work. Do we have the courage to stand up for the right and the true? Do we know what we are for? Do we have convictions? Some may have beliefs, but they are afraid to let the world know they are for them. Joseph of Arimathea and Nicodemus were secret followers of Jesus; they did not openly embrace Jesus as Lord because they were afraid of the Jews. Only after Jesus was dead did these two men have the courage to ask Pilate for his body and make preparations for the burial. Sort of late, wasn't it? In the Reformation period Martin of Basle was convinced of the biblical truth but was afraid to make a public confession of it. He wrote his beliefs on a parchment: "O most merciful Christ, I know that I can be saved only by the merit of Thy blood. Holy Jesus, I acknowledge Thy sufferings for me. I love Thee! I love Thee!" Then he removed a stone from the wall of his chamber and hid the parchment there. One hundred years later it was discovered. Contrast this with Luther who said, "My Lord has confessed me before men; I will not shrink from confessing Him before Kings."

There are some religious people who are firm and outspoken about what they stand for. While the mainline churches are declining in membership, the conservative churches are growing. Literalists, Fundamentalists, radical cults and sects are flourishing and drawing crowds. They are wrong at many points and can hardly be called Christians, but they know what they believe and why they believe it and they are willing to work and die for what they believe. At the same time, many Protestants are anemic in their faith, who know how only to ask questions about their faith, and express uncertainty and misgivings about eternal things. Here is the source of the weakness of Protestantism in our times.

If we are to stand, what do we stand for? We stand for plain, ordinary, and commonplace things, but things that are soundly biblical and absolutely true. We stand for the Bible as the Word of God. It is the book that God has written through inspired authors over the centuries. In this book God reveals himself. There you find the absolute truth about humanity and life as well as God and all eternal questions. The Bible has authority in matters of faith and life, and we hold that it is the only norm for faith and life. No other book, no other authority, no other organization has a superior word for our faith and life. Therefore, all things — thoughts and actions — must be in harmony with the teachings and spirit of the Bible.

We stand for the truth that we are saved by grace alone through faith. There is one way to God and the way is Jesus. In spite of the pluralism of our day, we hold that salvation is in Christ alone. This has been the faithful witness of the church since the apostles who preached that there is no other name under heaven by which a person may be saved except the name of Jesus. It is not enough to be a Jew to be saved; it is not enough to be a Buddhist or a Hindu or a secularist to be saved. We stand for the revealed truth that we are saved solely by the grace of God in Christ.

We stand for freedom. Paul urges us to "stand fast in the liberty wherewith Christ has made us free." This is one of our most precious gifts — freedom. Freedom from having to obey all the laws to be acceptable to God. We are free from all the rules, regulations, and ceremonies that men impose to be presentable to God. Through Christ we have freedom to be, freedom to live by our consciences, freedom to live out our lives under the guidance of God in everyday life. In this day of centralism and authoritarianism we need to keep standing for freedom by resisting every effort to subjugate us to man's rules, authority and suppression.

This certainly is what people today are wanting. They are crying out for some certain word upon which they can live. That is why conservative churches with an authoritative voice are growing. People will be drawn to Christ and the church when we Christians witness with a definite, clear, and certain message derived from biblical truth. Are you the kind of Christian that can give an intelligent and true answer to one who asks you what you stand for on the issues of today's world?

Stand on It

Here we stand. We stand against all ungodliness. We stand for the truth of God. Now we need to ask, on what do we stand! Where are you standing? Are you standing on the right thing and in the right place? A Navy seaman was held for tests after killing two hostages on a bus he hijacked from the Bronx to Kennedy airport. In response to a reporter's questions, he said, "I wish I wasn't standing here." Elijah must have felt that way when he was standing under a juniper tree and God asked him, "Elijah, what are you doing here?" Judas was standing in the wrong place when he betrayed Jesus, for Jesus asked him, "Friend, why are you here?" The first Psalm talks about a blessed man who "standeth not in the way of sinners."

A Christian stands on the promises of God. In the Bible there are more than 33,000 promises — plenty of ground upon which to stand! One of the most important promises is the one given by Jesus, "Lo, I am with you always." We stand on the promise that at all times and in all places God is with us to support and guide us. After the king had thrown three men of God into a fiery furnace, he looked in and found there was a fourth man like unto a son of man. The fourth was God with the men in the flames. When Paul was shipwrecked and panic broke out on ship, he addressed the men and told them not one would lose his life. He could say this because he told how there "stood by me an angel of God." Whenever God is with one person, there is always a majority. If God is with and for us, who can be against us? With this promise, you and I never have to walk alone through life.

Furthermore, we stand on the promise of God's grace for sinners like us. In John's first epistle we have the promise that "If we confess our sins, he (God) is faithful and just to forgive us our sins, and to cleanse us from all unrighteousness." That is one of the most precious promises to those who know they are lost and condemned creatures without any worthiness or merit. Think of that promise! You and I can be as low and dirty as it is possible to become, but when we repent and turn for forgiveness, there is a heavenly Father waiting to take us into his arms to forgive us. There is the gospel for you — the wonderful good news of a promise.

We stand also on the promise of victory in this life over all our problems. As we go through life, we sometimes think that we cannot make it. Everything seems to pile up; an operation for a possible malignant tumor, the wife is threatened with a still-born baby, the loss of job due to no fault of yours, an invalid father to care for, and on and on. It might be like the young minister about to start his ministry and his wife of three years tells him she wants a divorce. At a time like this, the promise of God keeps us from falling apart: "In everything God works for good to them that love him." The present may be bad but God will work it out for our eventual good. It is a temporary loss for a permanent gain.

Christians stand on the promises of God. Yes, but more so — on the solid rock of Christ. A hymn says it: "On Christ, the solid rock I stand, all other ground is sinking sand." This is an immovable rock, for Jesus Christ is "the same yesterday, today and forever." You can trust his word, for "Heaven and earth shall pass away but my words shall not pass away." Jesus is trustworthy. You can trust his word, his promises, and his guidance at all times and in all circumstances. So, we stand on him; we put our whole weight upon him. We trust in him for life now and for life through eternity. Pity the people who do not have this rock to stand on! That is why it is our privilege to share Christ with those who know him not.

You know, God expects us to do all we can to handle our life situations and to solve our problems. But, there comes a time when there is nothing more to do except to take a stand. This is the way it was with Luther when at Worms he said, "Here I stand. I cannot do otherwise. God help me." He wrote his books, preached his sermons, and consulted his friends. He did his best to persuade men of the truth of God as recorded in the Bible. What else could he do but to take a stand and trust God to work it out? When the Israelites left Egypt they were caught in a view: behind them were the Egyptians pursuing them and in front of them was the Red Sea. What could they do? Moses told them, "Fear not, stand firm, and see the salvation of the Lord." Stand and see God fight for you. After all, this battle for truth and goodness is not our battle but God's. While God fights for us, St. Paul urges us to "stand firm and hold to the traditions."

A Song That Says It All

God is our refuge and strength, a very present help in trouble. Therefore we will not fear though the earth should change, though the mountains shake in the heart of the sea . . . "Be still, and know that I am God. I am exalted among the nations, I am exalted in the earth!" The Lord of hosts is with us; the God of Jacob is our refuge. (Psalm 46:1-2, 10-11)

People seem to want to say all they feel and think in a song . . As a nation we stand at attention and sing the national anthem, "O say, can you see?" The alma mater of a high school or college is sung at special occasions to express the school's ideals and feelings. Lovers often have "our song" such as "I Love You Truly," and sometimes there is tension when the secular song is desired for the wedding. There is a hymn which for 456 years has expressed the faith of Protestants, particularly Lutherans. The words and music of Martin Luther in the hymn, "A Mighty Fortress is our God," say it all about the faith and spirit of Protestantism. Consequently, this hymn is found in practically every Protestant hymnal and since Vatican II is also used by Roman Catholics. Some claim that "A Mighty Fortress" is the greatest hymn ever written. It was found on the lips of dying martyrs. The whole army of Gustavus Adolphus sang this hymn as it marched into battle during the Thirty Years' War. The tune has been used by the world's greatest composers: Bach, Mendelssohn, and Wagner. Luther used the 46th Psalm as a basis for the content of the hymn. It is a hymn of affirmation, confidence, and trust in God as the ultimate victor over the world. The hymn is saying, "God is our refuge and strength, a very present help in trouble. Therefore we will not fear though the earth be removed. Be still, and know that I am God. The Lord of hosts is with us . . ."

If this hymn is so great, why do many of us find it hard to sing it with gusto? If this hymn sums it all up, why do most of us know only the first line, "A Mighty Fortress is our God," and not the four stanzas from memory? Even if we read the lines as we sing it, how many of us pay attention to the words? On this anniversary of Luther's birth, let us study this "Battle Hymn of the Reformation."

A Ferocious Enemy

When we sing "A Mighty Fortress," we are saying that we confront a fierce enemy. We recognize that there is a cosmic evil force. This evil is personalized in a figure called the devil or Satan. Since Christians and God are locked in battle with him, the hymn uses military language such as "fortress" and "bulwark." In this battle with evil, God is our fortress and bulwark. Take a look at the first stanza:

A mighty fortress is our God,
A bulwark never failing;
Our helper he amid the flood
Of mortal ills prevailing;
For still our ancient foe
Doth seek to work us woe;
His craft and power are great,
And, armed with cruel hate,
On earth is not his equal.

Luther describes the fierceness of this enemy. He is an ancient foe. His craft, his scheming and strategy, and his power are great. Notice what his weapon is: "cruel hate." And what is his goal? He seeks to work us woe. The devil is out to get us. He wants to ruin, destroy, and kill us. Luther says in this stanza that there is none greater than the devil on this earth.

Do we believe there is a real devil seeking to undo us? Or, is this some old-fashioned idea that has outlived its time? There are plenty of people who do not think there is any reality to the devil and hell. An engaged girl came home from a date with tears. Her mother asked what happened. The girl sobbed, "Tommy and I can't get married because he told me tonight that he does not believe in hell." Her mother comforted her by saying, "Now that's all right, honey. You just go ahead and marry him. Later you and I will prove it to him."

All around us we can find evidence that the devil is real, alive, and flourishing. The devil can exist in individuals. At Caesarea Philippi, Jesus recognized the devil in Peter when he said, "Satan, get behind me." One summer New York City was terrorized by a gunman who shot six women and wounded seven others. At last he was caught. He identified himself as "Son of Sam." When he was asked why he murdered these people, he said, "Sam told me to do what I had to do. I had my orders. Sam sent me. He told me to kill. Sam is the devil." Anyone who can murder six innocent young women must have the devil in him.

The devil can exist, of all places, in the church. His presence is seen by the church fights, the malicious gossip, the divisions and schisms that occur in a church. This is the work of the devil even in the holy precincts of the family of God. Sometimes the conditions in a church are so bad that one wonders how the congregation can call itself "Christian." Years ago a man bought a church building belonging to a black congregation. When the time came to give it up, the congregation failed to do so. Not wanting to take a church to court, the purchaser gave the church another thirty days, and then another thirty days. When his patience was exhausted, he rigged up a plan to get them out. While an evening service was in progress, he had a friend pull the main light switch and throw the congregation into total darkness. Then he pulled his car in front of the church for the headlights to shine through the window. He dressed up in a red devil suit and came throught the window in front of the congregation. The people jammed the exits in trying to flee the devil. One lady could not get out because she was in a wheelchair. She kept pushing backwards but the devil was gaining on her. When he got close to her, she said, "Now listen here, Satan, I want you to know that I have been a member of this church for forty years, a teacher of the Bible class for twenty-five years, and the president of the Ladies Aid Society for the last ten years. And I want you to know that I was on your side all the time."

Who can deny the existence of this evil power when we look at any daily newspaper? There is listed the work of Satan. Crime is the devil's doings. We have violence in terms of worldwide terrorism resulting in hijacked planes and the killing of hostages. Last year in America, arson, born of hatred and economic greed, destroyed a total of fifteen billion dollars' worth of property. We see the devil's presence in the sexual perversion of our times. There is a power that is seeking to destroy the church. Since the Communist take-over in Russia, ninety percent of the churches have been closed.

The Christian's Advocate

This is the terrible enemy Christians face in the world. How can we fight and prevail over an enemy so horrible? For a Christian to fight an enemy so powerful, it would be like a benefit fight held in Atlanta between Muhammed Ali and Jim Viandi, local TV sportscaster. Jim is just an average fellow and has no boxing ability or experience. The bout was a joke and it was funny to see Ali shadow-box and merely play with Jim. What chance does a Christian have against the devil? This takes us to the second stanza of "A Mighty Fortress."

Did we in our own strength confide
Our striving would be losing;
Were not the right Man on our side,
The Man of God's own choosing.
Dost ask who that may be?
Christ Jesus, it is he;
Lord Sabaoth his Name,
From age to age the same.
And he must win the battle.

This stanza gives us the good news that we do not only confront a terrible enemy but we have an advocate in Jesus. To win the battle with Satan, we do not rely upon ourselves but we look to Christ to fight the battle for us. He is the man of God's choosing and he is on our side in the conflict. Who is this Jesus? Luther gives his name as "Lord Sabaoth" and reminds us that Jesus never changes. Jesus must win the battle because God is greater and stronger than the devil.

In this cosmic conflict, Jesus is the victor over Satan. How did Jesus do it? It all began when God sent his Son on earth at Christmas. To fight the devil, Jesus had to become a man where he could meet Satan face to face for the combat. Jesus identified himself with man and was subject to all man's temptations from Satan. In humanity was the contact, the arena, for the battle. You will remember that Jesus was tempted in all points as we are except he did not sin. All through his earthly ministry Jesus struggled with the devil and won every battle.

Jesus won also when he was on the cross. Luther explains the cross as two opposing forces — God and Satan — meeting at the cross. Jesus was the bait God used to catch and destroy Satan. The devil swallowed Jesus and God caught him on the hook of the cross. On the cross the battle was won and Satan was defeated. Thus, Jesus gave a victory cry from the cross, "It is finished!" The strife is o'er, the battle's won.

The resurrection was the capstone of the victory. Jesus' rising on the third day was proof that on the cross Satan was defeated along with sin and death. And the last enemy of man is death and the reseurrection shows death is dead.

If Jesus won the conflict with the devil, how then is it that a war seems to still be going on? Why is the devil apparently alive and having great success with us? Why is sin more rampant than ever? The best answer is probably in the analogy of the Civil War. You know, the battle of Gettysburg was the decisive battle of the war. Though the issue was settled at that time, the war continued until Appomatox. Though the battles continued for awhile, the crisis was met at Gettysburg. The cross was the Gettysburg battle that decided the outcome. In our time the war continues and will continue until Jesus' return to earth. Then the Bible tells us Satan and evil will be utterly destroyed and Satan will be thrown into the lake of burning fire.

What does this mean to us today as we fight our battles with Satan? It gives us hope and confidence of eventual victory. We live with hope and confidence. Evil will not get us down. We are on the winning side of life. We shall overcome Satan and we are sure that Jesus will reign in the end.

One Word Does It!

But here we are on this earth and faced with this terrible enemy, Satan. Christ is not here to fight our battles. What can we do to fight off the devil and protect ourselves? Since Jesus is in heaven, are we at the mercy of Satan? In the third stanza, Luther deals with this problem:

And though this world, with devils filled,
Should threaten to undo us:
We will not fear, for God hath willed
His truth to triumph through us;
The prince of darkness grim,
We tremble not for him;
His rage we can endure,
For lo! his doom is sure,
One little word shall fell him.

Now we learn from this stanza that God has provided us with a weapon that is sure to defeat Satan. What do you think it might be? A high-powered rifle? How could this be if we, as St. Paul says, wrestle not with flesh and blood but against the prinicipalities and powers of wickedness? Without his parents' knowing it, a little fellow took his toy cap-pistol with him to church one Sunday moring. When they were not looking, he began to play with it as they sat in the pew listening to a sermon. All of a sudden the gun went off with a loud bang and everyone thought someone was shot. You can imagine how upset the congregation was and also how embarrassed the parents were. After the service a dear old lady came up the mother of the boy and said, "Now when you get home, don't you be too hard on the little fellow because he scared the devil out of more people this morning than the preacher has in ten years."

The weapon we have is the Word of God. Note the last line of the third stanza: "One little word shall fell him." One little word of the Bible will fell Satan. That is an amazing testimony to Luther's faith in the power of the Word. In and through that Word, God comes and turns the devil away. Jesus used this method when he was tempted in the wilderness. Each temptation was turned back when Jesus quoted from the book of Deuteronomy. The devil cannot stand the truth of God's word. He flees from the light of God's truth because he is the prince of darkness. This can be your weapon from day to day as you face the temptations of the devil. You need not say, "The devil made me do it." You cannot say, "I couldn't help it because the temptation was too great." You need not yield to temptation. You need not sin by yielding. You have "the sword of the spirit which is the word of God."

The Word can also turn away the devil when he afflicts us with despair. There is nothing like the Word to give us hope and courage to go on in spite of adversity. The great baseball player, Roy Campanella, was left a semi-invalid after an accident. In his autobiography, he tells of the turning point in his life. He says that when he was in the hospital, he lost all interest in life because he felt he was hopelessly paralyzed. He cried himself to sleep many a night. One day the doctor came in and asked the nurse to leave. He told him to stop feeling sorry for himself and that he was not the only one who had been hurt. He said, "Boy, you've got to fight. We can help you only ten percent. The other ninety percent has to be your effort." That shook Roy and he remembered how in the past he always turned to God for help. He asked his nurse to hand him his Bible and he opened it to the 23rd Psalm and read, "Though I walk through the valley of the shadow of death, I will fear no evil, for thou art with me." From that moment he was on his way back and he knew he was going to make it. The Word has power to drive away Satanic discouragement and despair.

If this is true about the Word, and we agree that it is true, then why do we neglect the Bible? If the Word is our weapon against evil, should we not read it, study it, digest it, and learn how to use it as a weapon? If the devil is having his way with us, maybe it is because we are neglecting to use the sword of the spirit, the Word of God.

You May Get Hurt

Thus far, we have seen that while the cosmic war with Satan has been won by Christ, the battles still go on between Satan and Christians. But, we have a God-given weapon that is sure to kill Satan, if only we would use it! The last stanza of Luther's hymn deals with the possible consequences of our fight with Satan. We may get hurt, and in this battle God is not promising us a rose garden of success and good luck. If you are going to fight, you can expect that you may get hurt or even killed. It is the risk that you take. For instance, suppose you get into a fight, as you probably did as a kid. When the fight was over, you could have had a black eye, a bloody nose, or a few teeth missing. When a man goes off to war, he knows that he might get injured or shot. That is expected in a battle. Some years ago the Veterans Administrator, Max Cleland, came to give an address on Emory's campus. He came and delivered his speech from a wheelchair. As you probably know, he is a Viet Nam veteran and lost both legs and an arm in the conflict. This is what Luther tells us in the last stanza of "A Mighty Fortress:"

> That word above all earthly powers,
> No thanks to them, abideth;
> The Spirit and the gifts are ours
> Through him who with us sideth;
> Let goods and kindred go,
> This mortal life also;
> The body they may kill;
> God's truth abideth still,
> His kingdom is forever.

Look at the price of fighting with Satan: "Let goods and kindred go" — property and family. "This mortal life also, the body they may kill" — and your physical being, the supreme sacrifice of your life. This may be strange to some because they think that if you believe in God, you should have everything good in life: success, health, and happiness. Dr. Quillian of First Church, Dallas, tells about a young fellow who came to see him the night before Palm Sunday when a group of young people was to be confirmed and received as adult members of the church. He explained that he needed to wait until the next class so that he could take the Confirmation course of study. But he lad insisted and begged and offered to take the course later. He just absolutely wanted to join the church the next day. Dr. Quillian gave in and agreed to receive him with his promise to take the classes later. While he was having breakfast Sunday morning, the same lad returned. When Dr. Quillian came to the door, the young man explained, "I just came to tell you that it did no good to join your old church because my dog died anyway."

Why should we expect skies always blue and flower-strewn highways through life when the faithful of the past had severe trials and sacrifices as believers in God? Daniel was thrown to the lions. Jeremiah was lowered into a pit and left to die. Peter was crucified upside down. William Tyndale was burned at a stake with a copy if his Bible hung around his neck because he dared to translate the Bible into the language of the people. The price of being a Christian warrior against Satan is to be the victim of the fray. You may lose your eyesight. You may get cancer and die an early death. If you truly lived as a Christian, you would soon get into trouble. You might be fired. Your friends might desert you. You may have evil stories told about you. Your family might break up. All kinds of things — bad things — can happen to a Christian simply because he is a Christian. But in this hymn Luther tells us it is all worth it. "Let goods and kindred go, this mortal life also, the body they may kill" — it is worth it because in the end God's truth remains and his kingdom is forever. Wickedness, sin, death, and the devil will be ultimately destroyed and Christ and his faithful will win, will reign forever in love and truth.

Did you realize there was so much in this great hymn? Can you see now why this hymn has been sung by milllions upon millions of people through the past four and one-half centuries? On this 500th anniversary of Luther's birth, we sing it again with confidence and strength. It sums up all that we as Protestants believe and feel. Every time we sing the hymn we affirm what the Psalmist wrote: "God is our refuge and strength, a very present help in trouble. Therefore we will not fear . . . the Lord of hosts is with us; the God of Jacob is our refuge."

Whatever Became of the Gospel?

I am astonished that you are so quickly deserting him who called you in the grace of Christ and turning to a different gospel — not that there is another gospel, but there are some who trouble you and want to pervert the gospel of Christ. But even if we , or an angel from heaven, should preach to you a gospel contrary to that which we preached to you, let him be accursed. As we have said before, so now I say again, If any one is preaching to you a gospel contrary to that which you received, let him be accursed.
(Galatians 1:6-9)

Five hundred years ago when Luther was born, it was a different world. Fantastic changes have taken place. This is the case not only in the world but in the church. In Luther's generation, Catholics and Protestants were at each other's throats as bitter enemies. Thanks be to God, that is not the case today. Since Vatican II, dialogues have taken place. Roman Catholics now are singing Luther's "A Mighty Fortrtess," and it is not unusual at Reformation services for a Roman priest to be the preacher. Some years ago this new climate became a reality to me. At a seminary professors' retreat in Chicago, the Communion bread and wine were administered by a Catholic priest. Later at a pastors' school, three of us constituted the faculty. One of the three was a Franciscan nun. In addition to teaching, I was the preacher at the evening services. Apparently touched by the message, the nun greeted me at the close of the service with a kiss. Did Luther turn over in his grave when a Catholic nun kissed a Lutheran pastor for preaching the Gospel?

But one thing has *not* changed. After 500 years the basic issue in the church is the same: the gospel. If Luther were alive today, he would ask, "Whatever became of the gospel?" In each generation the gospel is challenged. The war over the gospel is the same; only the battleground is different. As in our text, Paul fought the war for the gospel. For Luther the battlefield was the papacy. In our day the war is fought on the battleground of theological heresy. It is found not only in sects as Scientology and the Unification Church but even in our mainline denominations. Protestantism today is a battlefield for Fundamentalists and Liberals. Several denominations (Presbyterian, Episcopal,

Missouri Lutherans) have split in recent years. Almost half of today's Protestants in America, according to a recent survey, consider the gospel as "God's rules for right living." Does this reflect the lack of gospel preaching in our churches? Luther categorically declared, "Nothing but Christ is to be preached."

Why should we on this 500th anniversary of Luther's birthday be concerned about the gospel? Why is this an issue in our churches? Is it serious enough to give it earnest consideration? Yes, it is. At least Paul thought so. In our text Paul says that anyone who brings a different gospel other than the true one should be accursed. Another way of saying it is — he should be damned, let him go to hell! Paul is so moved and concerned about the true gospel that he repeats his threat: if anyone preaches a different gospel, let him go to hell. It is that serious. If you have lost the true gospel, you have lost everything worthwhile, because our Christian religion is built upon it. If you do not have the gospel, you do not have anything. Luther shared this view. For the sake of the true gospel, he was willing to lay his life on the line for it. That was the issue at the Diet of Worms. It was a false gospel taught by the church and the true gospel he found in the Scriptures. When ordered to give up the true gospel, he refused in the face of execution. He would rather die for the gospel than to sacrifice it. Thus, Luther said those immortal words: "Here I stand. I cannot do otherwise."

Half a God

At this time of celebrating Luther's 500th birthday, we seriously ask: Whatever became of the gospel? We ask it because various "different" gospels are being preached in our churches. For one thing, we are hearing a false gospel of a God limited to the world. Theologians call it the Immanence of God. It is a half-truth that God is in the world. The view is that God is not outside the world. They ridicule the idea that God is up there or out there. God came in Jesus and became a man, and since then God is in man, in the world, and in society. The Word of God is now the dignity of human flesh. God is the man upstairs. Jesus is our brother. We can pal around with God and talk to him in human terms, not in the reverential "thou" but in the intimate "you." This means that the transcendence of God has been lost. God is no longer the wholly other whose ways and thoughts are far beyond our ways. We have lost the greatness and grandeur of God. No longer are we impressed withthe majesty, glory and power of God. This is a dreadful heresy, because it has robbed God of his glory.

God of his glory.

This heresy has produced some unfortunate consequences in our midst. Now we have a God who is too small. This has ruined our prayers. Many of us have dropped the habit of prayer and we no longer put our trust in the power of prayer. Give us penicillin any day! God is not big enough, not powerful enough to answer our prayers.

Our God is too small to give us reverence, awe, and adoration in our worship. Today the church is in a worship crisis. People are not coming to church like they used to. Frantically we are being told to try experimental worship services, doing the far-out thing in the hope of attracting people. But they are miserably failing. There will be no improvement until we regain a God of majesty and glory before whom we will fall down in awe. Then there will be silence in our churches because God is in them. We will once more approach worship with a feeling of reverence for the holy.

The loss of transcendence has resulted in giving us an experience of the absence of God. God is supposed to be limited to the world, and now we cannot find him there. He is supposed to be in nature, but nature has curtailed our crops by too much rain, too much heat, and too much premature cold. The result is less food and higher prices. The average person cannot see God in that. God is supposed to be in humanity, but most people cannot see God in a Charles Manson, an Earl Ray, a Richard Nixon, a Spiro Agnew, or a Wilbur Mills. As a result, humans are experiencing a forsakenness and they cry, "My God, why have you forsaken me?"

If God's absolute, totally-other character is missing, then people have no absolutes by which to live. All is relative: morals, values, judgments. All is in flux and every person does his own thing. Each does what is right in his own eyes. Recently I served as supply pastor for a church. Behind the chancel where the choir met before the service, I had to go through a junk room to get to the choir. In this room I happened to notice a very old, dirty framed picture with this caption, "The Ten Commendments." At first I thought I misread the title, but a second look confirmed the printer's mistake. But it was a parable of our times. We do not have Ten Commandments without a God of holiness and glory; we only have commendments. We commend the commandments to you for your consideration. We comend the ten laws to you for trial. When God is truly God, the God of power, might, and majesty, we have commandments. These commandments came from God, are of God, and were written by the finger of God. They are absolute standards for life, because God gave them to us for obedience and a good life.

What is the true gospel about God? The gospel is that God is both immanent and transcendent. He is transcendent in that he is sovereign lord of all. God is not in nature; he is over nature. God is not in history; he is over history. God is not only in humanity but is over us. On the other hand, God is immanent. He is close and near to each of us. He can be closer than hands and breathing. The gospel is that God's presence in us is by the Holy Spirit. We do not naturally possess God. We must repent, believe, and be open to the Spirit. And when we receive the Spirit, we have God in us. And God can always be seen in people who have received the gift of the Holy Spirit.

A Singular Salvation

Moreover, we wonder what became of the gospel when we hear the heresy popular in our day that Jesus is just a savior of humankind. This is known as Pluralism. We are living in a pluralistic society. Anyting goes. You can do your own thing. One way is as good as another. This heresy is applied to religion. Christ is not *the* Savior of humankind; at best he *is* only a Savior. The thesis of this heresy is that it is not necessary to be a Christian to get to heaven. If this is true, then we need no Christ, no cross, no gospel, no church.

In fact, the heresy is that you really do not need a savior at all. You can work yourself into God's acceptance. This is the old heresy of works righteousness. It never wants to stay dead. Over and over the false gospel appears. And we all know it prevails among us. During the last two years Lutherans in America made a church-wide study of beliefs and discovered that two out of every five believe that they will be saved by their good works. It makes us preachers wonder what in the world we have been preaching all these years! You know it is a fact. Haven't you heard, or maybe you have said it yourself, someone says, "If I live right, if I do the right thing by my neighbor, if I do the best I can, I am sure God will take care of me." That is nothing but heresy, because the truth of the gospel is that we are saved by grace alone through faith alone and not of ourselves.

But, on the other hand, religion can save you, but it does not matter what religion it is. One is as good as another so long as you believe and are sincere. There is no question that a Buddhist, a Jew, a Hindu, or anyone else will get to heaven by virtue of his own religion. Christianity has no monopoly on salvation, they say. To think so is to be guilty of a religious supremacy. You are a bigot to think so.

The consequence of this heresy in our time has been disastrous for the spread of Christianity. If everyone is saved by his own efforts or by the religion he embraces, then there is no reason for evangelism or missions. In recent years church membership has plummeted. No longer are we sending out missionaries and those who come back are not replaced. Many think that to suggest to a person of another religion that he accept Christ is an insult and an affront to that person. They claim that the Christian thing to do is to let a non-Christian be happy in his own faith. Isn't it true that many of us share this heresy? When was the last time you witnessed for Christ? What do you care that the neighbors do not go to church or take their children to church school? You say that it is their business. If you believed that it is necessary to have faith in Christ to be saved, you would be concerned about the eternal welfare of that person's soul. You could not sleep at night because you know that Christ gave you the responsibility to witness and win that person for eternal life.

What is the true gospel about salvation? In the gospel there is no pluralism; it is all singular. The Bible tells us there is only one God; all other gods have no real existence. There is only one Son of God. There was but one cross and one full and final payment made for the sins of humankind. Paul says over and over: one, one, one, one, one. One faith, one God, one Christ, one baptism, one Lord. Jesus taught that no one came to the Father but by him. The Apostles preached that no one is saved except by the name of Jesus. The last thing Jesus said was that the Disciples should go into all the world and make disciples of all nations. There is no other way to eternal life, no other way to heaven, no other way to get right with God. One God — One Christ — One way: repent and believe in the Lord Jesus. Now that is the true gospel and if anyone says anything else, Paul says in our text that person should be damned.

The Glory of Man

Whatever became of the gospel? We ask that question because we see there is a heresy which makes humanity the center of life. God has been removed from the scene. Humanity has taken the place of God. This is called Humanism: man-at-the-center of life. Now we hear men speak about and we read about "the glory of man." Man is everything these days. We are told that we should prize ourselves as human beings. We have integrity. The *summum bonum* is to be a person. We are urged to be human and to act like human beings. If it is so important to be human, then we need to learn our self-identity. The big craze of our time is self-understanding. The truth is that we should rather be learning to know God and then we would know who we are. We ought to be spending our time learning to understand God and then we would understand our creatureliness.

The consequences of this heresy is that we have a false view of humanity. We think that we are naturally good. We are saying to each other in the title of a best-seller, "I'm OK — you're OK." There is nothing wrong with us that education or good business will not cure. In you, they say, is great potential. Get to know yourself and let your best self come forth and you will have power and success. Rev. Ike explains, "We only attempt to convert the individual to himself . . . to believe in himself correctly and positively and to realize unlimited possibilities of the presence of God in him."

If we are OK, then we are by nature good. We have no sin to confess or of which to repent. This is shown by the decline in the practice of confession of sins in our churches. Many churches do not bother with a confession of sins in the order of worship. At one time Lutherans had a special confessional service on a weekday in preparation for Communion the following Sunday. This was dropped for a lengthy confessional service prior to the Communion. This made the service too long. We then prepared one that was only a paragraph long. Now we use a watered down version of confession in "Celebrate," and we do not realize that we have confessed our sins. This is a far cry from the publican who beat his breast and cried, "God, be merciful to me a sinner."

It is true that the modern person has done some great things and made wonderful progress. What we can do today is what a former age would call miracles. In spite of such scientific progress, we are basically helpless and lost. We can walk on the moon but we have not learned to walk with God on earth. We have extended the span of life from 47 in 1900 to 74 in 1974, but we have not learned how to make life worth living. We can speak from one end of the world to the other in a minute, but when we talk we have nothing important to say. We can build machines to fly, as the recent Air Force plane flew across the Atlantic, faster than the sun, but when we get there, we do not know what to do with ourselves. We should not be proud, for we do not know the answer to cancer. We are at a loss to know what to do to solve inflation. We had better humble ourselves before God.

What is the true gospel about human beings? It simply says that apart from God, humans are a lost and condemned creature. Apart from God humans are beasts and brutes. There is nothing but deceit in the human heart. The natural person is a lost person. That is what the Bible says. Humans were made good but they rebelled against God and became bad and have been bad ever since Adam. The gospel is that we need to be remade, to be converted, to be transformed. We need to become new creatures by the power of the gospel. Thus, every person needs to repent and turn to Christ.

When we do repent, we become children of God by grace through adoption. Now we are somebody because of what God does for us. We are now precious and of inestimable value because of the price God paid for us in the blood of Jesus. Now we have an inherent worth, a precious value, a sun-crowned brow, and we walk with the dignity of a born-again child of God. As a partner of God, as an instrument of God, we have infinite possibilities to do good and to be good.

In recent years the church has been busy trying to find its purpose in the world. Each congregation is urged to have a self-study to find out what it is supposed to be and do. Isn't that strange that we must study to find out what we are here for? Is it not obvious that we are as stewards of the mysteries of the gospel? We have been given this treasure. We are here to believe in the gospel, to value it as most precious, to love it, to defend it, and to proclaim it. This is our pearl of great price. Thus, we take our stand in behalf of the true gospel. We cannot do otherwise than to die for it if necessary. God help us!

The Danger of Being Religious

But this is the covenant which I will make with the house of Israel after those days, says the Lord: I will put my law within them, and I will write it upon their hearts; and I will be their God, and they shall be my people. And no longer shall each man teach his neighbor and each his brother, saying, "Know the Lord"; for they shall all know me, from the least of them to the greatest, says the Lord; for I will forgive their iniquity, and I will remember their sin no more. (Jeremiah 31:33-34 Reformation Sunday)

Two young boys were close friends. The one asked the other to come to his church. Although he declined to go, the friend insisted that he go with him to his church. Finally the lad said, "I can't go to your church." "Well, why can't you?" asked the friend. "Because," he answered, "I belong to a different abomination."

Religion can be an abomination. Have you ever stopped to think that the greatest and best people were victims of religion? The prophets, like Jeremiah who gave us our text, were persecuted by religious people. Jesus was crucified by the scribes, Pharisees, and Sadducees, religious leaders of the day. John Hus was burned to death by church authorities. The church excommunicated Luther who considered the head of the church to be antichrist. John Wesley was shut out of the churches, even his own father's church. In our time religion has done some terrible things: the poisoning of more than 900 in Jonestown, Guyana, under the leadership of a preacher, Jim Jones. The clergy leaders of Iran executed several thousand opponents of their regime. The assassination of Egypt's Anwar Sadat was carried out by religious fanatics. Apparently Jesus knew the danger of religion when he said, "Beware of false prophets."

Because of its human element, religion can deteriorate to where it is a curse to humanity. As we celebrate Luther's 500th birthday, we are reminded that the purpose of the Reformation was to cleanse and reform the church of false teaching and moral corruption. What happened to the condition of religion in the sixteenth century also took place in the sixth century B.C. when Jeremiah lived. The religion of Judah was in a deplorable condition. It was so rotten that God told Jeremiah that it should be discarded and abandoned for a new religion, a new covenant.

God inferred that the old religion of Judaism was too far gone to be repaired, reformed, or rejuvenated. God promised Jeremiah that he would make a new start, give Israel another chance, and inaugurate a new deal in religion. It would be God's kind of religion, a true religion that would be a blessing to all people. In our text we learn what the elements are of this religion, the way religion ought to be.

A Personal Religion

God's kind of religion is a personal religion. Thus, he says in our text: "I will put my law within them, and I will write it upon their hearts; and I will be their God, and they will be my people." You cannot get more personal than that, can you? The law of God is to be in people. God himself will write it on the table of the heart. And there is a personal relationship: "I will be their God and they will be my people."

An unworthy religion depersonalizes people. This kind of religion makes us think more highly of things than of people. Years ago a man had a habit of going out before breakfast to get a pitcher of water from the pump in the backyard. One morning he slipped on the ice and landed with a bang. His wife heard the noise of his fall and called to him through the kitchen door, "Henry, did you break mother's blue pitcher?" In pain he responded, "No, I didn't, but I *will*." Thereupon there was heard another crash! It is like a teen-ager calling to say he was in a car accident. The first question his father asks, "Any damage to the car?" The youth gathers his father is more concerned about the car than about his physical welfare. Why didn't he ask, "Are you hurt?"

The church today can be guilty of this. We often put primary emphasis upon buildings, budgets, and programs. People seem to come in second in our concern. A church is considered a great success not for the number of people served but for the size of the church plant and the half-million-dollar annual budget. This is not God's kind of religion where people come first.

Moreover, we tend to depersonalize our religion by forgetting the individual. Jeremiah said that God would write the law on each person's heart. There is a tendency for the church to get busy with more important projects than a single person, one individual. Julia Ward Howe was once talking with Charles Sumner, the distinguished senator from Massachusetts. She begged him to help a certain person. The Senator replied, "Julia, I've become so busy I can no longer concern myself with individuals." She responded, "Charles, that is quite remarkable. Even God has not reached that point yet." Some of us in the church minimize and overlook the individual in place of numbers. How we love to boast of our church attendance! According to some, bigger is always better. This was not Jesus' way. For him religion was a one-to-one relationship. The lost 100th sheep was as important as the ninety-nine which stayed in the flock. He emphasized that God knew even how many hairs were on each head, and of the billions of people on earth, God even knew your name as one person. The Bible tells us that we as individuals are graven on the palm of God's hands. If religion does not begin with the individual, it does not begin.

True Christianity is a personal religion, because it is based upon and is centered in Jesus Christ. Christianity is not a principle, policy, or program. It is a personality. The Word became a person in Jesus. No one can be a Christian until he/she has a personal and intimate confrontation with and commitment to Christ. From the beginning, people have become Christians through a personal experience with Jesus whether it was Paul on the road to Damascus, Augustine in his garden, St. Francis at a shrine, Luther in the Black Tower, or John Wesley on Aldersgate Street.

In the sixteenth century the church had become depersonalized. Luther and other Reformers worked and sacrificed to give the church back to the people. In Luther's day, the church was an autonomous hierarchy which had full control and authority in all matters. At best, the people were to be obedient and faithful servants of the church. For one thing, the people were deprived of the Bible. It was in the Latin language which most people could not read nor understand. Actually the Bible at Luther's time was on the list of forbidden books. The church said, "We'll tell you what is in the Bible, and we only can interpret it for you." This caused Luther and other Reformers to translate the Bible into the language of the common person so that every person could read the truth of God for him/herself. To this day, the Protestant church is known as the church of the open Bible for the people to read. Yet, the irony of our times is that while the average home in America owns four Bibles, very few people read it.

In the area of worship, the people at best were spectators at the mass. The people had no part in it. They were told to use their rosaries for personal devotions while the priests went through the mass. Luther was convinced that this was not true worship. He claimed that every Christian has the need and the duty to thank and praise God. Accordingly, he translated the mass into the vernacular and reformed the mass to enable people to participate in the liturgy. Luther was one of the first Reformers to write hymns, such as "A Mighty Fortress," that people could praise God by their singing. Some of us have negated our worship heritage by coming to church as spectators only and to be entertained by choir and preacher. No person truly worships unless there is participation in the service and the hymns are heartily sung.

In Luther's age, the people had little or no part in prayer in terms of direct communication with God through Christ. The church taught that the ordinary person was unworthy to go directly to God in prayer. A person needed intermediaries — priests, saints, martyrs, and the virgin Mary — to intercede for him/her. Luther brought back prayer to the people by teaching the biblical doctrine of the priesthood of believers. It simply and rightfully claims that every Christian has the right and privilege to go directly to God through Christ without the benefit of any intermediary. The gain was made at great cost to the Reformers, and yet we take prayer so lightly and casually as to neglect the privilege of prayer. Whatever your need, whatever your problem, whatever your sin — take it to the Lord in prayer. The Christian religion is for you as a person and for all of us as people. True religion, according to our text, is a personal religion.

A Truthful Religion

According to God's Word in our text, a true religion is a truthful religion. Listen again to our text: "And no longer shall each man teach his neighbor and each his brother, saying, 'Know the Lord,' for they shall all know me, from the least of them to the greatest." In this new religion of God's, every person will know the truth of God for and by himself. It will not be a truth learned by rote, nothing you get in a classroom, but an intuitive, God-disclosed truth.

To know the truth is not an easy thing. Pilate asked Jesus, "What is truth?" Most of us sit in Pilate's seat. We do not know the truth of God and we are subject to partial views of the truth or we embrace what is not the truth. One time two beggars were approaching a house to ask for food. In the front yard was a huge dog who with bared teeth growled and at the same time wagged his tail. The one beggar was afraid to go to the front door. His associate said, "Don't be afraid. The dog is wagging his tail." "Yes", replied the other, "I see that, but I don't know which end is the truth."

The Reformation was a period when Luther and the Reformers proclaimed the truth of God in opposition to the established church. The people were not hearing the truth. They were taught that a person is saved by accumulating merit through doing good works: buying indulgences, attending masses, and going on pilgrimages. The Reformers rediscovered the truth of God in the Scriptures: by grace are you saved by faith. A person is justified by faith. The truth was summed up in the motto: "Grace alone, faith alone, Word alone." To this day the Protestant church is based on and lives by that truth.

In our times, we are faced with sects and cults that are not teaching the truth of God even though they claim the word "church." Today we have a Unification Church founded some years ago by a Korean, Sun Myung Moon. According to their "Bible," "The Divine Principle," it is taught that Jesus was prematurely killed before he was able to marry and have a model family. Since God's plan was frustrated, it is taught that God sent Moon as the Second Messiah who is the Lord of the Second Advent. He and his wife claim to be the model family of God. According to the Scriptures, this is not the truth.

Then there is in our day the Church of Scientology founded by a science-fiction author, Ron Hubbard, in 1950. It is a religion of psychotherapy and self-improvement by mind manipulation. It is taught that each person is an immortal spirit, a Thetan, which at will can separate from the body as a supernatural being. According to the Bible, this teaching is garbage.

There is another religion popular in our day. It teaches that the state and church are instruments of the devil. Thus, they refuse to pledge allegiance to the flag and to serve in the armed forces. The established churches also are the work of Satan and ministers are his agents. A former student of mine, a Methodist minister, called me long distance some time ago with sobs to tell me how crushed he was when his daughter, having fallen in love with a Jehovah's Witness, would not allow him to marry her because he was allied with Satan. Nothing is farther from the truth!

We have a "church" that denies the reality of sin, sickness, death, and hell. They claim that these ideas are only figments of imagination. Certainly, this is a half truth.

You may be asking, "How do we know we have the truth of God? Where can one get the truth?" It is a good question. The truth of God is recorded in the Bible. For this reason we say that it is the Word of God. In the Scriptures God reveals himself and speaks to us the word of truth. "But," you say, "there are so many teachings in the Bible. Which ones should we accept?" The answer is in Christ. The truth of God is incarnated, impersonated, and personified in Jesus who said, "I am the truth." Christ is the whole and ultimate truth of God. We need look no farther for greater truth. God's last word is Christ, the perfect revelation of the Father. Again, you may protest that the truth as Christ is too broad for us to know the truth. The church comes to our rescue with the ecumenical creeds: Apostles, Nicene, and Athanasian. Since the first century, the church has summed up the whole truth of the Bible in the short paragraphs of the creeds. For these twenty centuries, Christian people have been reciting the creeds as an adequate summary of God's truth revealed in the Scriptures and personified in Christ.

It is tragic that people by the droves are leaving the mainline churches, particularly young people, for the sects and cults that are misleading people by their false teachings. The reason for their success in attracting our people is our failure to properly teach our children and youth the truth of the Scriptures. If there is anything urgently needed in our day, it is a wholesale return to our church schools where our young would learn what we believe as Christians and why we believe it. Having the truth of God, they will not fall victim of the sects and cults that are a plague to truthful religion.

A Liberating Religion

God's kind of religion, the kind we should have, is a liberating religion. God says in our text: "I will forgive their iniquity, and I will remember their sin no more." God in a true religion forgives and forgets! Now that is good news for us! It is a liberating religion — free from sin, free from guilt, free from hell, free from condemnation, free to live and laugh and love!

Modern people ought to be for this kind of religion, for we love freedom. When the American hostages were released after 444 days in Iran, a mother in Edwardsville, Pennsylvania, ran out to the main street clanging a cow bell wildly, and shouting, "My Bruce is free! My Bruce is free!" Everywhere people are yearning to be free from oppression. Some flee Communism by hijacking planes, or flying over borders by balloon. Some brave the Pacific or the Caribbean to get freedom in America.

False religion enslaves people. In the sixteenth century, the people in the Roman Church were enslaved by false teachings and the hierarchy of the priesthood. They were bound to work out their own salvation by obeying the laws of the church and by earning their way to God's acceptance by good works. They were held captive by the church's teaching of Purgatory, and they were urged to buy indulgences to shorten the time in Purgatory. In a fifteenth century church in Germany, there is a framed notice still to be seen in the sacristy that promises people who say the Lord's Prayer five times will get 30,000 years off their stay in Purgatory.

In our century, we still have religion that enslaves by literalism and legalism as well as fundamentalism. In cases like these, religion is a burden and a curse. It is a religion of rules and regulations: Don't do this and Don't do that! Recently a serviceman was given an honorable discharge because he refused to roll up his sleeves when ordered because he claimed his religion forbid him to unduly expose his body when women were present. There is a Fundamentalist college in Greenville, South Carolina, that forbids its 6,000 students to drink, smoke, dance, date a person of a different race, wear brief clothing, listen to Billy Graham, and attend a Southern Baptist Church. Recently a thirteen-year-old girl was raped by a group. She caught VD and became pregnant. She wanted an abortion but her mother did not approve because it was against her religion. This is putting people into a moral straight-jacket. To say the least, it is confining and curtailing the freedom of a person in the name of religion. Granted, there are some people who like these rules. They want to be told what to do and what is right. This relieves them of having to make decisions. Even though it is false, they like security. But, it is an easy cop-out in living a free, moral life.

Contrast this with the freedom we have in the Christian religion. We are free from having to make things right with God, for Christ has already done this for us. We are free from having to fulfill the demands of the law, for Christ fulfilled all the laws for us. We are free from guilt because of God's gracious forgiveness. There is nothing we have to do or give to gain God's favor. There are no conditions to be met before God accepts us. It is not "if" we are good, "if" we are obedient, "if" we are faithful, God will forgive us. No, it is not in "if" but in "because." Because God loves us, because Christ died for us, because God wills all to be saved, we are made children of God. That means we are free to be ourselves, to enjoy life, to live as in God's presence, and free to live, to laugh, and to love.

Now, every one of us needs to be religious. It is not a matter whether we are religious, but what kind of religion we have. For surely we have learned by this time that one religion is *not* as good as another. There is nothing worse than bad religion and there is nothing better than the true Christian religion. Here is the danger of being religious: we may have the wrong religion. So, the question gets down to this: do we have a false or a true religion? In our text Jeremiah puts it this way: Are we living by the old covenant of the law or by the new covenant of grace in Jesus Christ?

Are You OK With God?

Since all have sinned and fall short of the glory of God, they are justified by his grace as a gift, through the redemption which is in Christ Jesus, whom God put forward as an expiation by his blood, to be received by faith. (Romans 3:23-25a)

In recent years there has been a popular book by Harris entitled, *I'm OK — You're OK.* It is a book about transactional analysis which calls for a harmonious relationship between persons resulting in both being able to say, "I'm OK, You're OK." This book has found much favor in our churches and has been used extensively in some churches.

There is a deeper relationship that has been omitted. A more basic question is, "Are you OK with God?" If you are not OK with God, then you cannot be OK and I cannot be OK. My relationship with myself and my relationship with you depend upon a right relationship with God.

"Are you OK with God?" refers to the biblical teaching known as Justification by Faith. It is the central teaching of the New Testament, the cardinal doctrine of the Protestant church, and a basic question of each person. The answer to the question, "Are you OK with God?" is found in our text. Since Paul, it has been the key teaching of the Christian faith and was rediscovered by Luther in the sixteenth century. It is said that each one of Luther's thousands of sermons in some way dealt with the theme of Justification by Faith.

Most of us today do not understand the term, "Justification by Faith." We put it in different terms by asking, "Are you OK with God?" This is the basic, fundamental question every person asks. How can I get right with God? What must I do to be saved? What will make me acceptable to God both now and through eternity? These are questions that apply to each of us here and now. It is not an academic question of the first or the sixteenth centuries. The question is personal and immediate: "Are you OK with God?"

I Am Not OK With God

What is your answer? Apart from Christ you can say that you

are not OK with God. By your natural state, by simply being a human being, you are not OK with God. Why not? It is because of the nature of God. In our text Paul says that we "fall short of the glory of God." The glory of God reminds us of the perfection, the justice, the majesty, and the holiness of God. And what does this kind of God expect of us? He expects us to be no less than he is. Peter quotes Leviticus when God says, "You shall be holy, for I am holy." In the Sermon on the Mount, Jesus taught, "Be merciful, for your heavenly Father is merciful . . ." "Be perfect as your Father in heaven is perfect." When Jimmy Carter confessed to *Playboy* magazine that he lusted after women, his wife, Rosalyn, tried to make excuses for him by saying, "Jimmy was only saying that God does not expect a man to be perfect." That is not true. God does expect a person to be perfect. God cannot stand sin. He is a holy God. To be in God's presence, to be OK with God, one must be godly, just like God. If we are not perfect, holy, and godlike, then we are accountable to God and we are subject to his judgment and his wrath.

There is another reason why you and I apart from Christ are not OK with God. It is due to human nature. Our text says that "all have sinned." Who can deny this? Have you ever met a perfect person? One time a pastor asked this question of his congregation. Not expecting an answer, the pastor was surprised when a man raised his hand. He said, "You have known a perfect person? Who was it?" The man replied, "He was my wife's first husband." We can laugh at that because we know full well that every single person is far from perfect. This is true not only of the common man or woman but even the very best, high-ranking people whom we expect to be better than the average. We see it is the case with our top political leaders. Jimmy Carter in the presidential campaign told the nation through *Playboy* magazine that he lusts after women. Former President Ford admitted he made a mistake in the campaign debates about the countries of southeastern Europe. Betty Ford said she would understand if her daughter had a pre-marital sex affair. Shall we mention Richard Nixon or Spiro Agnew or John Mitchell? Some of our top religious leaders are also guilty of sin. Malcolm Boyd, nationally known Episcopal priest, recently admitted to the press that he was a homosexual. Last year the news media reported that a French cardinal had a heart attack and died while visiting a prostitute. A leading Florida clergyman a few weeks ago shocked his city when he killed his wife and son. Even St. Paul would put himself in this condition, for once he said, "Christ died for sinners of whom I am chief."

You are not OK with God, also, because of the nature of sin. Is sin important or is it an old fashioned idea? To God sin is a terrible thing, for it marks rebellion and disobedience. What does sin do? It is a wedge that separates God from man and man from man. Anyone of us can understand this from daily experience. When some unkind word is said or a dirty deed is done, we know how frosty the relationship immediately becomes. We will not talk to each other. If we see the enemy coming down the street, we will cross the street to avoid meeting him/her. The more we sin, the farther we get away from God. As we sin daily, we get as far from God as the east is from the west. Sin blinds and blinds us to all that is good and true. We get so entailed in sin that we become helpless and hopeless. As a result of sin, we make for ourselves a hell on earth. This is a hell of a condition to be in. That is why Paul in Romans cries out in utter despair, "O miserable man that I am! Who will deliver me from this body of death?" This is the normal reaction of everyone who is not OK with God. This makes us raise the question again and again, "How can I become OK with God?"

I Am OK With God

How to get OK with God has been humanity's perennial question. All of the answers can be summed up in three simple attempts. One way is the way of self-effort. It can be compared with steps. You know that to go up a step you must use your own energy and strength to pull yourself up to the next step. As you get older, the steps get harder, because you no longer have the strength you once had as a youth. The idea is to go up the moral staircase, one that stretches from earth to heaven. Each step represents a virtue. The logic is that if we can be as good as God, we will be OK with God. That makes sense and that is true. The problem is making yourself morally perfect.

The trouble with the idea is that it is not only difficult but impossible. Who can climb a staircase that extends from earth to heaven? My office is on the fourth floor and when I get to the top floor, I am panting like a horse that has galloped at full speed for a mile. Each year it is getting harder to climb those stairs. It is as impossible as someone saying to me, who can just about swim the distance of a swimming pool, that I must jump in the ocean off the Atlantic seaboard and swim across to Europe. In his autobiography, Benjamin Franklin tells how he tried to make himself morally perfect. He began on one virtue until he mastered it. Then he went to the second. Later he began working on the third, but by that time he found that he broke the first virtue. He finally gave it up as a bad job!

Are any of us still trying this method of becoming OK with God? Today the book market is flooded with self-help manuals. One of today's best sellers is Dyer's *Your Erroneous Zones*. Others in great demand are entitled *How To Be Your Own Best Friend*, *The You That Could Be*, and *You Can Cope*. These books are being bought by the hundreds of thousands who think that by applying postive thinking they can be the person they think they ought to be. There is many a person who believes that he must do better or God will not love him. He talks about having to shape up and do better. If we live right, we are supposed to go to heaven. Who has not heard the remark at a funeral: "I know he is in heaven because he was a good man." In a magazine article an Atlanta rabbi wrote, "Salvation is not unearned, unrelated to human effort, a gracious gift of Heaven. It is the achievement of people in a world ruled by a God of justice and love. Redemption will not descend from heaven, it will be won on earth. Its source is not beyond history. Its stage is the arena where people live, struggle, aspire, worship, fail, suffer, repent, and achieve salvation."

Even if we were able to perfect ourselves morally through climbing the steps to heaven, we still would not change the inner core of man. And that is where the real problem is. Sometime ago on the 11 p.m. news telecast, the camera showed a gathering of 300 people watching a trainer put a lion through his tricks. He was supposed to be very harmless. They said he was de-clawed. The lion was thought to be so harmless that the trainer asked a spectator to join him in the cage and help him put the lion through his tricks. The time came when the lion was made to lie down. Then the two men sat on his body. The trainer stood up and as the spectator rose, the lion went after him, clawing and biting him. They had to rush the man to a hospital where he received forty-eight stitches on his face. The "calm" and "harmless" lion turned back into a beast. It is the same with us. Through self-effort we can refine ourselves. We can be trained to act nicely and courteously. We can secure a veneer of civilization with all of our culture. But, inside the heart there is still the beast that unexpectedly strikes out of us and shows the world what kind of a nature we really have. Our moral problem goes to the heart and we will never be what we ought to be until God gives us a new heart and a new spirit.

Someone in north Georgia played a dirty trick on a man who raised lions by opening the gate for the lions to escape. They went into the hills of north Georgia. The police came with guns to get them. Since they were dangerous, they turned down the suggestion that they be shot with tranquilizers. They rejected the idea of trying to catch the lions. For them there was but one answer: Shoot them! And so they did, every one of them, and the people of north Georgia once more felt safe and secure. And that is the only thing that must be done with the beast in our hearts. The beast must be killed. The New Testament puts it in another way. It says that the old Adam in us must die that the new man in Christ might live.

The Escalator to Heaven

The idea of getting OK with God by climbing the moral steps through self-effort is an impossible possibility. Is there another way to get OK with God? There are those who think they can get OK with God by doing their very best and then asking God to give them some help to reach the goal. This may be compared to an escalator. It will take you to the height you want to go without any effort on your part. But, did you ever see a person on an excalator being dissatisfied with the speed of the escalator and start to climb the escalator while it was still running? He seemed to say that he needed to help the escalator get him where he wanted to go. Or, did you ever have the experience of getting on an elevator with a person carrying two heavy bags? He does not put them on the floor of the elevator but holds them with the thought that it would make the load lighter for the elevator. There is something inside us that makes us want to do our part to get right with God.

This principle is based on the idea that "God helps those who help themselves." In some things this may be true, but when it comes to getting OK with God, it is another impossible possibility. We say that it is a "possibility" because we can become OK with God if we perfect ourselves into a state of absolute holiness that God can accept. It may not be a bad idea to get a little divine help on the side to do this. Not only is this impossible for us to reach moral perfection with only a little help from God on the side, but it is so absolutely unnecessary. God alone can make us fit to be in his presence. He will do it all. He wants to do it all. In theology this attempt to work along with God to become acceptable is known as synergism, a working with God. For centuries the medieval church taught that man is not saved by faith alone but by works and faith. You did what you could and then you sought God's aid through the sacraments of the church. This was so untrue according to the Bible that when Luther translated the Bible and came to the place where it said that man is justified by faith, Luther added the word "alone." But this was really no addition because the context implied that it was by faith alone that man is made right with God.

Even if it could be true that we cooperated with God in our salvation, our part would be infinitesimally small, a barest minimum that would add up to zero. Once a father and his five-year-old son were working in the garden. The father filled his wheelbarrow with dirt. When it came time to move it, the little fellow said he wanted to wheel it. The father let the boy believe that he did it. The boy put his hands on the handles but behind the boy was the father who with his sinewy arms and strong back pushed the wheelbarrow to its destination. The boy thought he did it all, but all he did was to lay his hands on the handles. He probably did more harm than he did good. No, walking up the escalator of self-help plus God's supplementary aid is no way to get OK with God.

The Elevator of Grace

Our text gives us the one and only way to get OK with God. It is a matter of free grace through Jesus Christ received by faith. Paul expressed it this way: They are justified by his grace as a gift, through the redemption which is in Christ Jesus, whom God put forward as an expiation by his blood, to be received by faith. In other words, we become OK with God by means of an elevator. God uses as a shaft of the elevator the long arm of the cross extending from heaven to earth. Christ is the "car" that comes down the shaft to earth through the Incarnation at Christmas. The believer accepts Christ and Christ lifts him up to the cross-arm of the cross, on a level with God. Now God sees us as sinners with Jesus at our sides as our Mediator. Our sinfulness is covered with the red robe of Jesus' perfection. For Christ came to earth to be man, to obey all of the laws man was expected to obey, suffered and died for the sins of man, died in man's place. He rose in glory and returned to the Father. Now God sees not the ugly, dirty sinner but he sees the perfection of Jesus surrounding the sinner. For Jesus' sake, God forgives, pardons, accepts, and loves the sinner.

What did we do to get OK with God? We did nothing, because the elevator of grace did it all. In an elevator you do nothing but stand. The elevator lifts you up. The chorus of a gospel song says, "Love lifted me, love lifted me. When nothing else could help, love lifted me!" In place of the words, "Love lifted me," you can sing "John 3:16." It explains what that love is. John 3:16, according to Luther, is the "little Bible." It contains the gospel. Atlanta now boasts the highest hotel in the world, seventy stories high. You can walk into the lobby and get an elevator to take you to the top. Can you guess how long it would take to get you to the top? It takes only one and one-half minutes to go up more than 700 feet. And what did you do to get that height? If man can do this with an elevator, just think what God can do with his cosmic elevator that takes us from earth to heaven to be with God — and we did not do nor deserve anything to get lifted! That is grace!

But, an elevator can go up and down for eternity and will mean absolutely nothing to you unless you get on the elevator. To step on an elevator requires faith. If you were afraid of an elevator, you would not get on it. It takes faith to take an elevator because you must believe it is safe and that it will take you to your desired height. In the same way, it takes faith in Christ to get OK with God. You must believe in Christ, believe he is able to make you OK with God, believe that you are safe in his hands. When you step on the elevator of Christ, that is what is meant by "accepting Christ."

Did you ever notice that you cannot go half-way into an elevator? You cannot put one arm into the car and say that is as much as you will trust. You cannot stick a leg through the doors and try that much of the elevator. If you are going up, you must go as a whole person. This means that faith calls for total self-surrender. You must give your whole self to Christ in trust. The Hebrew word for trust is "batah" which means throwing oneself forward. When you go into Christ's elevator, you throw your whole self upon the mercy of Christ; you put your whole weight on God. You just simply turn everything over to God and let him take care of you.

Isn't this wonderfully good news? Are you not excited and grateful for it? Doesn't it want to make you jump for joy? Look what God has done for us in Christ! He lifts us up to himself and we did nothing but to trust him in faith. This is the gospel. It is good news. Did you ever notice the name of your Lutheran church? It is not simply a Lutheran church, but is called, for instance, "The Evangelical Lutheran Church of the Redeemer." The word "evangelical" means "good news" in Greek, the gospel. Don't ever remove that word from your title because it is what makes you a Lutheran church, yes, a Christian church. Cease to be evangelical and you cease to be a true Christian. In the light of the elevator of grace, by which we are made OK with God, we have reason to rejoice and to celebrate. Behold, look what God has done for us in Christ!

But what have we been saying? It is simply that without Christ you cannot be OK with God. With Christ you can be OK with God. It is as simple as that. The key to the situation is Christ. Thus, the matter of getting OK with God depends upon who and what Christ is to you. It is said that soon after Dwight L. Moody received his call to preach, he was advised to go to England and Scotland to consult famous preachers how he should preach. He interviewed one great preacher who was not much help to him and he was about to leave. The famous preacher called him back, had him take a seat close to him, laid his hand on Moody's knee, looked into Moody's eyes and asked, "Are you O and O?" Moody did not understand and asked him to repeat. Again the preacher asked him, "Are you O and O?" Moody confessed he did not understand. The preacher then said, "Are you out and out for Jesus?" How is it with you and Jesus? Are you, too, out and out for Jesus? If so, you are OK with God. Then and only then can you truly say, "I'm OK." But, are you OK?